CASSETTE CULTURES

Past and Present of a Musical Icon

JOHN Z. KOMURKI
LUCA BENDANDI

BENTELI

CASSETTES ARE BACK!

THE RISE, FALL AND RISE OF THE COMPACT CASSETTE

Back in 1995, science fiction writer Bruce Sterling called for a book documenting 'dead media' – all those obsolete devices and platforms, from the astrolabe to the zoetrope, that were once cutting-edge but have since fallen by the wayside in the march towards technological perfection. "What we need", Sterling wrote, "is a somber, thoughtful, thorough, hype-free, even lugubrious book that honors the dead and resuscitates the spiritual ancestors of today's mediated frenzy. A book to give its readership a deeper, paleontological perspective right in the dizzy midst of the digital revolution".[1]

In one sense, *Cassette Cultures* represents another volume in a dead media encyclopaedia. An icon of 20th-century culture, technology and design, the cassette tape redefined how music was listened to and shared. The different cultures it enabled and sustained around the world had a radical impact on communication itself. But there is no doubt that tape's golden era is long over, and that it will never again attain even a fraction of the prominence it used to enjoy.

But the music cassette is actually very far from dead. In fact, it is enjoying a renaissance that would have been unthinkable even a decade ago. How and why did this happen? What lies behind the resurgence of a format most people had all but forgotten? What is the evergreen appeal of the humble compact cassette? This book is an attempt to answer these questions, and in the process trace the as yet unwritten history of this generous format. In doing so, we will see that the tape is still the foundation of a living and dynamic tradition, and that, barring a brief blip when everyone was infatuated with digital media, there is a sense of an unbroken continuity between the first people to innovate with the cassette as a musical format, the pioneers of 'cassette culture', and the many people all over the world today who continue to use it as a tool for creativity and community-building.

Of course, this movement is not without its critics: "At best, the cassette revival is merely a vacuous fad of no genuine value; but at worst, it's a confused, regressive cultural misstep", as one commentator put it.[2] More than hipster nostalgia or analogue fetishism, however, this book is about celebrating cultures that continue to bind and inspire, as well as a technology that remains relevant to our understanding of how media work. Freed from the drudgery of serving the mass market, it might even be the case that tape is now more fully itself than it ever has been. When a new technology arises, it possesses a "utopian dimension", in the words of one philosopher, which it loses over time as it comes to serve as a mere commodity. However, "it is precisely at the moment of the obsolescence of that technology that it once again releases this dimension, like the last gleam of a dying star. For obsolescence, the very law of commodity production", the same philosopher continues, "both frees the outmoded object from the grip of utility and reveals the hollow promise of that law."[3] For obsolescence, then, read apotheosis.

We are today able to evaluate the cassette with clear eyes, no longer in the dizzy midst of our first obsession with the digital. This book is a celebration of how the cassette still holds a prominent place in the contemporary media sphere, as well as the Valhalla of forgotten formats.

TAPE STORY

THE INVENTION THAT MADE MODERN MUSIC POSSIBLE

"Magnetic tape opens the door", wrote John Cage in 1955. It "introduces the unknown with such sharp clarity" that old habits are "blown away like dust".[4] It may be hard for us today to get a sense of the impact tape had, of which doors it opened and which habits it blew away, when it first hit the mass market in the 1950s. One area in which it had a defining influence was music, of course, particularly in terms of broadcasting and recording. Radio shows had previously only been broadcast live, but they could now be pre-recorded or aired more than once. And, while it had only been possible to record music in single takes, multiple versions could now be recorded and then recombined. Writing in 1966, musician Glenn Gould talked about "the splendid splice", referring to the way that tape enabled him to record different takes and then cobble together the best bits of each one.[5]

In essence a medium for storing and retrieving data, magnetic tape's basic principle of operation remains largely the same as it always has been. Tape constitutes a long, thin strip of plastic film, made of a durable and flexible substance like PVC or Mylar. The whole strip is coated on one side with iron oxide or chromium oxide: this is the side that records data. Most tape players have a recording head and a playback head. When recording, the tape rubs against the record-ing head, which applies a magnetic field to the tiny, needle-shaped iron oxide particles the tape is coated with. This field is based on an input signal (derived from whatever it is you want to record) and it lines up the magnetic particles in a certain pattern, not entirely un-like what a magnet does to iron filings. Now, when the recorded tape rubs against a playback head, the same input signal is reproduced as output, as the aligned particles transfer the same magnetic pattern to the head.

HISTORY AND FACTS

BEFORE CASSETTE

1928

Magnetic tape for recording sound was invented in 1928 by Fritz Pfleumer, a German-Austrian engineer.

1935

Pfleumer's invention was developed by the German corporations BASF, who worked on the tape, and AEG, who worked on the device, releasing the world's first tape-based recorder, the Magnetophon, at the Berlin Radio Show in 1935. After the Second World War, the Americans snaffled the technology, prompting a wave of innovation. In 1958, RCA announced that they had developed a tape cartridge that could record 30 minutes of sound, the immediate precursor of the tape cassette.

Never before has a car radio done this

Philips Cassette Car Radio plays <u>your</u> choice of music too!

It's a quality car radio. And a cassette-player too. In one simple unit the size of a car radio alone. First of its kind in the world. A great idea!

You can select stations on long and medium waves. Hear them loud and clear. Or insert a Musicassette and hear *your* choice of music. Anytime. Anywhere.

Musicassettes are quality recordings on tapes sealed in slim cassettes. No scratches, no dust. Music can't be erased.

Hundreds of titles available, from pop to classics. And there's a special Philips Musicassette Car Collection available if you purchase a Cassette Car Radio.

Ask your dealer to demonstrate Philips RN582. Yours for **38 gns** (recommended price) suitable for 12-volt negative to earth only.

POST TODAY for brochure and details of special

Please send me details of Philips Cassette Car Radio.

NAME..

ADDRESS..

PHILIPS

1963

Compact Cassette

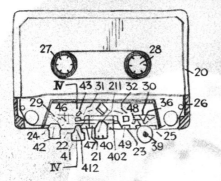

27 28
20
IV 43 31 211 32 30
29 46 48 36 26
24 25
42 22 47 40 49 39
41 21 402 23
IV 412

The first incarnation of the cassette as we know it today was launched by Dutch tech giant Philips in 1963, also at the Berlin Radio Show. Originally intended for use in dictation machines, the Compact Cassette was the fruit of a long process of adapting clunkier and less reliable tape technology to a domestic context. The breakthrough was to encase the delicate magnetic tape in a sturdy and portable plastic container, the cassette. In order to guarantee its spread, Philips shared manufacturing rights with whoever wanted them, as long as they followed Philips' specifications. Several other companies promptly started producing this new "music maker for the masses", and the format became a hit across the world.

1966
1967

The first cassettes were released in the US in 1966 (with albums by Nina Simone and Johnny Mathis, among others) and in the UK in 1967. One key reason for its early success was that nearly twice as much music could be recorded on a tape than on a record – a 33-rpm record could hold about 22 minutes per side, while a cassette held 45.

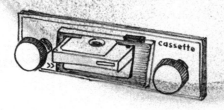

cassette

The cassette proved particularly popular with teenagers, also a relatively new invention at the time, as it meant they could listen to their music in their cars, one of the few spaces that young Americans had to themselves.

Left:
1968 ad for the first Philips car radio that could play cassettes, highlighting the features of the medium.
Private collection.

Subsequent milestones included the adaptation of the Dolby noise reduction system for cassettes in 1969, reducing hiss and increasing dynamic range, and 1970, the year that the Radio Corporation of America first noted that cassette sales had adversely affected record sales.

Tape technology was so prominent and important in the music-recording industry that for a while sound and tape were almost synonymous. One symbol of this is the 8-track, which was a central music-making tool throughout the '60s and '70s, despite being rather finicky to work with. Following this period, the increasing availability of magnetic tape-based technology enabled people to record, produce and release their own music, sidestepping every kind of middleman.

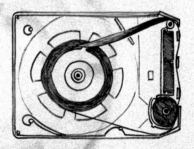

The late '70s saw TASCAM and Fostex release 4-track tape decks with built-in mixing boards. Inexpensive and portable, these were a major boost to bedroom studios. Alongside synths and drum machines they made it possible to create professional-quality recordings with a lo-fi intimacy. Bruce Springsteen, for example, seeking to make a 'pure' album, recorded his *Nebraska* album on TASCAM. Gary Numan, Soft Cell and Daniel Johnston were other well-known aficionados of the technology. In short, as the technology improved, magnetic tape became more and more widespread as a musician's tool.

Tape is highly versatile, and it came to have a transformative impact across a range of fields besides music. One of these was information technology. Tape was used for data storage on 1950s mainframe computers. Later, in the first days of home computing, when floppy discs were still prohibitively expensive, many computers could interface with normal audio devices in order to store data on audio cassettes. Apple II, Commodore 64 and BBC Micro could all use cassette tapes for storage, and a range of commercial software could be bought on tape.

The Commodore Datasette was an example of a dedicated tape-based storage device, which took the form of an adapted consumer-model tape recorder. When recording on a blank tape, you would fill out the inlay card as you would any mixtape, with the meter reading on the tape drive alongside the titles of programmes or games. In fact, Sony and IBM are still today innovating with tape as a storage medium, partly due to its longevity relative to digital storage formats.

© Rob Fraebel (2018)

Television signals are similar to audio signals, and another field where tape was constitutive was that of film and TV, particularly in terms of domestic consumption and production. Various tape-based video formats competed to corner the market, but in the end VHS won the format war and became the pre-eminent home video format – until the advent of the DVD. A curiosity: the PXL-2000, a black-and-white camcorder produced in 1987, that used a compact audio cassette to record both sound and image. Marketed as a children's toy, it was a flop on the market and only 400,000 units were ever produced. However, its grainy, lo-fi effect became popular with avant-garde filmmakers and something of a cult has grown up around it, with models today selling for up to $500.

1987

DAT

Attempts had been made to integrate digital and tape-based technology. One was the Digital Audio Tape or DAT, released by Sony in 1987. Looking like a normal cassette but shrunk to half the size, the DAT sampled and reproduced sound digitally, and there was thus no loss of quality when producing subsequent tapes – it didn't make a copy so much as a clone. The DAT was intended to replace the compact cassette, but for different reasons it never really caught on outside professional circles.

1982

COMPACT disc

The compact disc or CD, a format premised on the digital recording of music and data, was first commercially marketed in 1982, and by 1988 CD sales in the United States (ever the bellwether for musical formats) had overtaken those of vinyl LPs. In any case, tape's days were numbered by the early '90s. In 1992, for the first time more CDs were sold than pre-recorded cassettes.

For a while tape and CD co-existed side-by-side like Neanderthals and Homo sapiens. During the LP's wilderness years it was quite common to have a music collection that mingled CDs with cassettes, typically recordings of other people's CDs. Then – almost overnight – it became possible to burn music onto CDs, robbing tapes of their most primal function.

So it was the cassette's turn to go into the wilderness, while people dusted off their vinyl and installed CD players in their cars. Today, however, just about the only place people still listen to CDs is in their cars. Tapes, meanwhile, have learned from vinyl's example and followed it back into the mainstream.

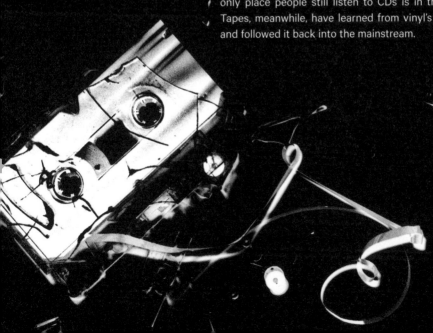

THE BOOMBOX
& THE WALKMAN

Today we take it for granted – wherever we are, we're listening to our music. But there was a time long before the days of online streaming when your music collection stayed at home, shackled to a hi-fi. Then, in quick succession, two devices came onto the market and together precipitated a revolution in personal listening. Thanks to the boombox and the Walkman, people became able to curate a mobile soundtrack to their lives.

Both these iconic appliances were based on cassette technology. But they embodied opposed musical habits. The boombox was noisy, brash, extrovert. It turned music outwards, for all to love or hate. The Walkman was quiet, withdrawn, introvert, enveloping users in a self-enclosed aural universe. For the first time in human history, enjoying music became an insular, solitary activity. As well as comprising a potted history of pop culture, the story of these two revolutionary devices shows how the cassette changed listening forever.

The boombox was the weapon of a whole generation.[6] A design icon and a music machine unparalleled in magnificence, it was a potent symbol for disaffected urban youth: Run DMC, the Beastie Boys and the Clash were among many groups to adopt these oversized radio cassette players as totems.

Previous page:
Weapons of a Generation
lettering by Federico "Tails".

The world's first boombox was the Philips Radio Recorder, released in 1969. But the boombox is really a testament to Japanese industrial design, emblematic of the revolution in Japanese manufacturing that took place in the 1970s and '80s, as the sector became more and more innovative (the strength of the dollar against the yen meant that these high-end products were widely accessible in the US). Many of the most well-loved boomboxes, among them the Sharp VZ-2000, the JVC RC-550, and the Panasonic RX-7000, were Japanese-made.

Left:
LL Cool J carrying his JVC,
New York City, 1985.
Photo by Janette Beckman.

Each boombox had its own look and feel. They all had a handle and took batteries, making them fully transportable. Some models even had leather pads so it could perch comfortably on your shoulder. Many were reinforced in some way, adapting them to street life. All were extravagant in appearance: covered in chrome and glossy plastic,

WALKIN' DOWN THE STREET TO THE HARDCORE BEAT WHILE MY JVC VIBRATES THE CONCRETE

LL Cool J – 'I Can't Live Without My Radio' (1985)

This Panasonic stereo has one component your component system doesn't have.

A handle.

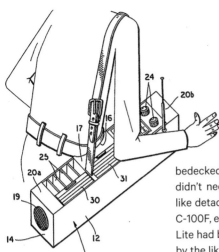

24
20b
17
16
25
20a
19
31
14
30
12
11

Detail from the patent for a portable music device.

bedecked with dials, buttons, meters, knobs, and flashing lights, they didn't need to be playing to make noise. Some featured gimmicks like detachable speakers or keyboard synthesizers. One, the Conion C-100F, even came with a motion detector alarm, while the Vela Disco Lite had built-in flashing light bulbs (as seen in various music videos by the likes of Madonna and Lady Gaga).

There is also a range of sonic identity across different models, with sound and fidelity being key. Released in 1978 and for many the archetypal monophonic boombox, the JVC RC-550, aka 'El Diablo', had a 10-inch woofer, as well as a four-inch mid-range, a two-inch tweeter, and separate bass and treble controls. To make room for it all, this model is so big the tape deck looks tiny.

In the 1986 film *Peggy Sue Got Married*, Kathleen Turner is transported 25 years into the past. In the future, she explains at one point, "for some reason everything else gets tiny, but portable radios get enormous". There always was something confrontational about the boombox. One of its primary functions was to invade space, to aggressively reclaim the aural landscape. This was one reason for its popularity among some marginalised urban populations in the USA – the boomboxes became a way to have presence and autonomy in an environment rendered hostile. The term 'ghetto blaster' came to be used variously with disdain and with defiance.

The boombox embodies a mode of sociability that is different, even opposed, to the individualistic values typical of contemporary global capitalism. It is all about the street, coexistence, communal culture. Its opposite is the Walkman. If the clichéd vision of the boombox is of a group of brightly dressed kids breakdancing on a New York street corner, the Walkman evokes a 1980s salaryman gazing blankly at his own reflection in the window of a crowded metro carriage, orange earphones clamped to his head.

Left:
Composition based on a vintage Panasonic ad for a boombox, highlighting one of its most revolutionary features: the handle.
Private collection.

WALKING STEREO with HOTLINE
WALKMAN

ど、キリリと締まった濃紺の小さなボディ。小意気なヘッドホンを通じ、低音から高音にまでクリアに
ステレオ。●ふたりでサウンドを聴きつつ、ヘッドホンを通じ会話ができる、ホットライン機能付。
"連続再生約8時間を実現したコアレスモーター。●歩きながらでも、安定したテープの走行を

TPS-L2 ¥33,000

SONY
STEREO

From the moment it was launched in 1979, the Walkman revolutionised many aspects of daily life, from a workout at the gym to the morning commute. As ever, its first cheerleaders were teenagers, eager to tune out the world.

There is no doubt that the advent of the Walkman was a key moment in the history of modern music technology. But more than that, it transformed our relationship to urban space. According to Shuhei Hosokawa, first theorist of the Walkman, the device changes the street into a living theatre: "The Walkman makes the walk act more poetic and dramatic. It enables the quasi-complete separation of the audible experience and the visual one of a pedestrian... We listen to what we don't see, and we see what we don't listen to... [The Walkman] will make the ordinary strange..."[7]

Then there was the French sociologist who was so perplexed by this invention that in 1981 he hit the streets to interview Walkman users: Are you losing contact with reality? Is the relation between sound and

Graphic elaborations on period advertising. *Private collection.*

vision radically changing? Are you psychotic or schizophrenic? But one respondent coolly interrupted him, telling him his questions were out of date, a hangover from previous generations' understandings of communication. The youth, in short, were unfazed, seeing this new technology not as an existential disruptor but simply an expansion of their possibilities of freedom.[8]

Compact and stylish, the first Walkman is a design classic (it's the one Star Lord has in *Guardians of the Galaxy*): a 14-ounce, blue-and-silver model with chunky buttons, a second earphone jack (so two people could listen at once) and a leather case. Today mint-condition original pieces can fetch thousands of dollars. When they first released it, Sony already had a track record of producing sleek, miniaturised electronics. The marketing of the early models of Walkman played an important role in introducing a new vision of Japanese design to the world – elegant, diminutive, hi-tech.

The legendary TPS-L2, the first Walkman. *Image courtesy of Hugo Rodriguez, The Walkman Archive.*

Right:
Graphic elaboration on period advertising. *Private collection.*

Following pages:
The Walkman Hall of Fame. *All images courtesy of Hugo Rodriguez, The Walkman Archive.*

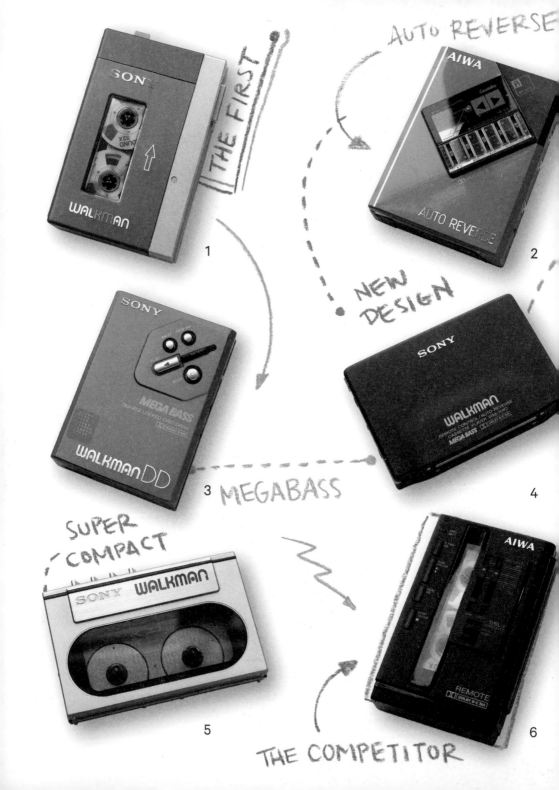

THE FIRST

AUTO REVERSE

1

AIWA

AUTO REVERSE

2

NEW DESIGN

SONY

WALKMAN DD

MEGA BASS

QUARTZ LOCKED DISC DRIVE

3 MEGABASS

SONY

WALKMAN

REMOTE CONTROL / AUTO REVERSE
CASSETTE PLAYER WM-701C
MEGA BASS

4

SUPER COMPACT

SONY WALKMAN

5

AIWA

REMOTE

6

THE COMPETITOR

BEST SOUND QUALITY

RECORDING PERFORMANCE

7

8

9

LUXURY

DYNAMIC OPTIMIZATION

10

The Walkman Hall of Fame according to The Walkman Archive

01 SONY TPS-L2
02 AIWA HS-G8
03 SONY DD30
04 SONY 701C
05 SONY WM-10
06 AIWA PX-101

07 SONY DD9
08 SONY D6C
09 AIWA JX3000
10 SONY Boodo Khan
11 SONY WM-F5 Sports (following page)

SPLASH PROOF

The name Walkman was inspired by the machine that it was based on, a journalist's portable radio called the Pressman. At first the company had doubts about the name, fearing it sounded too Japanese. Walky and Disco Jogger were floated as alternatives, but in the end Walkman stuck, giving rise to one of the most controversial linguistic debates of our time: is the plural Walkmans or Walkmen? Sony actually tried to cut this Gordian knot with 'Walkman personal stereos', but no one was convinced.

Walkman was the king of the '80s. Other brands like Panasonic and Toshiba got in on the craze with their own versions, and their runaway success surely played a part in the ascendance of the cassette. In 1986, 'Walkman' even entered the Oxford English Dictionary ('cassette player' was recently removed, by the way).

The high-water mark of Walkman's success came some time late in the decade. Brands carried on innovating, with additions like bass boost, AM/FM radio, and auto-rewind. They even produced a solar-powered model. But the appearance of the CD marked the beginning of the end for personal cassette players. While Sony were quick to shift their focus to the Discman, and indeed continue putting out MP3 players, they have never been able to recapture the quintessential stylishness of the Walkman.

by Max Poser, My Radio Berlin

After collecting boomboxes for over 10 years, I have come across quite a few models that had left something to be desired despite promising great performance and sound. When you are new to this world, finding an affordable model that suits your needs is not an easy task. Where do I look for used vintage cassette players? What do I have to look out for? How much money should or can I spend?

Unless you live close to a store that sells vintage electronics or know someone who still has an old cassette radio, you probably want to consult eBay if you are looking for a wide range of choice. If you live in a big city, classifieds are also a great resource. If you were expecting to find decent models in working condition at a flea market, I have to disappoint you. In 10 years I have probably taken home three or four boomboxes from flea markets that ended up working. You might find that lucky once-in-a-lifetime deal, but chances are you won't.

Look at as many listings a possible. Since everybody has a different idea of nice design, go through a couple of listings and think about what aspects you like (round speaker grills, symmetrical layout, buttons on the front or on top, etc.). One manufacturer often uses very similar designs throughout a variety of radios; the Sharp GF series, for example. Try to come down to a style you prefer and look out for listings that fit your criteria.

Decide which functions you want and need. Of course, there are portable powerhouses like the Sharp GF-777 that come with all the features you could possibly desire in a radio cassette recorder, but those features come at a higher price. So you have to ask yourself which of those switches you would use on a regular basis. One thing that I strongly recommend is getting a model that has separate bass and treble controls or a graphic EQ instead of a single knob for tone control. A loudness switch is something I also like to have on boomboxes. It basically amplifies the bass and treble end and is very useful at lower volumes to make the unit sound richer. In terms of look,

Previous pages:
Vela DK-990R: a model built in 1986. Its "Personal Disco Component" makes it unique by adding lights that flash along to the rhythm of the music. Madonna and Lady Gaga featured The DK-990R in their music videos.

This and following pages: Images courtesy of My Radio Berlin.

you definitely want some VU meters, either bouncing needles or flashing LEDs. Not only do they look great when you are listening to music, they are also extremely helpful if you want to record cassettes on your device.

Speaking of cassettes, if you want high-quality playback and recording make sure the cassette player has a chrome/metal selector and Dolby noise reduction or something similar. The wattage of the boombox does not really tell you a lot about its sound. Some of the cheapest and worst-sounding radios claim to have 100 Watts and some of the very good-sounding and high-end ones are advertised as having 20 to 30 Watts. What you should rather look for is a two- or three-way speaker system (four or six speakers). Some models also have a RCA line-in that is very handy to plug an external device like an MP3 player into the boombox.

Avoid complex tape decks. The kind of deck that is least prone to break out of the blue is a mechanical deck, on which you physically press the heads up or down by pressing a key. There is a certain directness to this that is very enjoyable, much like placing a stylus on a record. Then there are soft-touch decks. While they are usually of good quality, they tend to get stuck if the main drive belt is weak. Most of the time this is a simple mechanical fix that just requires a new belt. Logic-controlled decks can develop more serious issues as you do not engage anything mechanically. These types of decks are usually the toughest ones to repair.

Make sure to buy a fully working device. It sounds simple enough, but sometimes one can forget to read the full description and end up getting a defective boombox. Unless you are handy with electronics or know someone who is, you are basically stuck with a large paperweight. Most repair places are specialised in more modern technology and getting a vintage boombox fixed by a professional can cost a fortune.

Finally, be patient. Watch the market or wait for the model you want. There are models that are quite rare and others that are not so rare but are still high quality. If you are not sure, don't buy it. Just wait and you will eventually find your perfect boombox.

If you are on a middling budget, the M70 is the box for you. It is probably the best-sounding mid-sized boombox that was ever built: big,
mechanical tape keys, dual VU meters, very solid two-way speaker
system. It leaves almost nothing to be desired.

If you want even better sound, check out its big brother, the RC-M90, as featured on album covers by LL Cool J and the Beastie Boys. Be prepared to pay four to five times as much for it as for an RC-M70, though.

The best boombox Sharp ever built, hands down. This one is more of a portable recording studio than a boombox. Two very reliable soft-touch decks are paired with a three-way dual-amp speaker system. The GF-767 is almost identical but does not have as many features.

The C-100F features two tape decks, LED and needle VU meters, a tape run display, and even a spare tape drawer at the bottom. The three-way speaker system is second to no other model when it comes to volume. Understandably, it is very sought after, and getting one in good shape is not an easy or inexpensive task.

A *compact cassette*

000 I had a cassette about Princess Di. It was lovely. A series of interviews with her, but it also walked through some of the day-to-day visits she had to do. The one that stuck with me, for whatever reason, was when she visited some kind of traffic marshal, who explained how they programmed traffic lights in London. Seemed terrifically mundane. But I enjoyed listening to it. **023** When I was doing singing lessons as a boy, my teacher used to record my voice, then we would listen to it straight away, cringe, and then sing the part again. **048** Well, since then there has been a lot of talk about piracy, but for years we all pirated like crazy! That was a main advantage, along with portability. And there were the custom mixes, the cassettes recorded by the biggest music lovers, which everyone else copied. **064** I discovered that when the tape unspooled, you could wind it back in using a pencil. I thought this was a very intelligent solution and I was surprised no one else had ever thought of it. **075** I remember that my father, after we emigrated to Canada, recorded the phone calls he made to my grandparents, who lived in Italy. He used to connect a device (a microphone) to the stereo and record these phone calls, and then listen to them to hear the voice of his parents.

B memories mix

121 My godfather sent me the *Hitchhiker's Guide to the Galaxy* on cassette and I would listen to it before I went to sleep. I loved the hiss at the end of each side, the pink noise. Very relaxing, like rain. I think that's the origin of my obsession with experimental music, actually. **164 I've worked in clubs for 30 years. I sold over 850 different cassettes. I had hundreds of masters of all the national and international DJs. 243** I remember once when I was a teenage boy driving past Frankfurt on the autobahn with my dad. He put his old beloved Pink Floyd tape on. While the atmospheres of the album got thicker and thicker he put the volume to the maximum, something he never did, and his foot pressed more and more heavily on the pedal, until the Volvo accelerated to a speed I did not know the old motor could handle. He looked forward, his eyes wide with surprise. For a moment it felt as if the superior power of music had taken over the steering wheel. **310 All the extraneous noises. The clunky buttons, the sound of a tape going round, the slightly worrying rattle if you shook the thing, the sort of squeaking noise it made as you wound it on with your finger. 375** You couldn't steal them from Woolworths, because they just had empty boxes on the shelves. And yet I can't in all honesty say we never stole those empty boxes.

As a well-known meme
has it, the youth of today
have no idea that these
two objects once shared an
intimate, almost symbiotic
relationship.

WEGERT

90 (2×45) Min.
LOW-NOISE

A

CaSSETTE
CuLTuRE

Borrow it.

Use it

give it back

Most tape players are inherently hybrid, in that they can both record and play, produce and reproduce. The domestic tape player likewise created a new type of hybrid user, both producer and
consumer: a new breed of creative, reconstructive music lovers.
Before tape hit the mass market, music (like culture in general)
had always been pre-mediated. Nominal authoritative figures
(DJs, critics, etc.) would decide what you should listen to, and woe
betide you if your tastes fell anywhere between the lowest common denominator and the highest common factor.

Thanks to the cassette, however, people found themselves able
to produce something that was functionally identical to the 'real',
formally produced thing, but at the same time an undiluted expression of their own personality. Suddenly, everyone was a DJ,
able to express themselves through sound, unreservedly, cheaply,
and with no prior experience.

REPRESSIVE USE OF MEDIA	EMANCIPATORY USE OF MEDIA
Centrally controlled program	Decentralized program
One transmitter, many receivers	Each receiver a potential transmitter
Passive consumer behaviour	Interaction of those involved, feedback
Production by specialists	Collective production
Control by property owners or bureaucracy	Social control by self-organization

To conceptualise the new freedoms that tape enabled, it can be useful to think in terms of an opposition between "emancipatory" cassette culture and traditional ("repressive") media, as summarised in the scheme on the opposite page.[9]

It's worth highlighting here that the 'culture' part of 'cassette culture' was the key thing – the format itself was just a means to an end, with none of the mystique that some tape fans today see in it. In fact, many people thought cassettes in themselves were rubbish: truculent, time-consuming and unreliable. What was exciting about them was the access they granted to interactive, 'emancipatory' networks.

IF YOU DON'T LIKE IT. DUB OVER IT

Tape also expanded the freedoms available to musicians. As we've seen, cassette-based technology made it possible for bands to record and produce their own music in home studios, freeing them from the need to make demos in by-the-hour professional studios or court the attention of gatekeepers. Cassettes, in short, are great liberators of expressive potential. As pioneer Eugene Chadbourne wrote years ago, "the most common point of view is: 'Who gives a shit? If you don't like it, dub over it.' And after more than a decade documenting my music that's the most exciting thing I've heard".[10]

Left:
The differences between "emancipatory" cassette culture and traditional, "repressive" media. Quoted in Peter Manual's *Cassette Culture: Popular Music and Technology in North India* (1993).

The advent of the double (hence 'dub') cassette recorder was one of the factors that made possible this new approach to musical creation. "To use the language of Jamaican reggae and dub, you just 'version' it", wrote Dick Hebdige in his *Cut 'n' Mix* (1987). "And anyone can do a version. All you need is a cassette tape recorder, a cassette, a pair of hands and ears, and some imagination."[11]

C·30 C·60 C·90 GO!

BOW WOW WOW

TC·EMI 5088
℗ 1980
(Original sound
Recording made
Moulin Rouge
Ltd.)

SUN SEA AND PIRACY – BOW WOW WOW
All rights of the producer and of the owner of the recorded work
reserved. Unauthorised copying, public performances and
broadcasting of this record prohibited.

2

100   50   0

BOW WOW WOW

□□ DOLBY SYSTEM ®

OFF THE RADIO, I GET A CONSTANT FLOW
HIT IT, PAUSE IT, RECORD IT AND PLAY
TURN IT, REWIND IT AND RUB IT AWAY

Bow Wow Wow – 'C30, C60, C90 Go' (1980)

C30. C60. C90 GO

Even if you only recorded songs off the radio, this was already a fundamentally empowered and creative act, a way to reshape culture and define yourself in relation to it. In this, the cassette anticipates many aspects of contemporary sonic life. Artist Mike Bouchet has observed of the VHS, the cassette's first cousin, that "Our collective ability to analyse different eras of film stocks and video qualities, cognitively follow extremely fast edits, not to become nauseous from handheld footage, and simply form consensus on how well a commercial has been made is all due to our cultural conditioning to video".[12]

Can we make a kindred assertion about tape? Is our apparently automatic ability to move fluidly in a world of MP3s and online streaming, of endless, seamless, idiosyncratic recombinations of music, a skill that was made possible by a collective familiarity with the cassette, and with the possibilities it engendered?

The original release of Bow Wow Wow's subversive classic 'C30 C60 C90 Go!'.
Private collection.

Early cassette enthusiasts emphasised connectivity, and the possibility of building non-hierarchical, decentralised relationships around the world. In his essay 'The Cassette Underground', tape theorist Steve Jones defined cassette culture as "a vast international network of musicians and music fans who create and consume music via cassettes... largely in opposition to the traditional music industry".[13] He was writing 30 years ago, but his definition still rings true.

One important reference point in the nascent cassette culture was *OP*, a US-based experimental music magazine, which in its fifth number started a column called Castanets, featuring reviews of cassettes and the addresses of their producers. Like an analogue Soundcloud and Facebook rolled into one, people used the column to reach out to other tape obsessives and set up exchange circuits that spanned the globe.

Various covers of the ground-breaking experimental music magazine *OP*.

LOST MUSIC NETWORK'S

Op

NDENT MUSIC
MAGAZINE

Op

Op "K" Issue, May-June 1982 $1.50

LENNY KAYE/HENRY KAISER/
/TOSHINORI KONDO/DAGMAR K
/KARL & INGRID BERGER/
KYTHNOS/"KOSSUTH"/
ROLAND KIRK/JIM KATZIN/
KRALDJURSANSTALTEN/
NANCY KARP/KNEBNAGAUJE

A KALEIDOSCOPIC ARRAY OF
KINKY CONTACTS & KEEN REVIEWS

Lenny Kaye

ISSN 0276-8747

Op

The "F" Op Summer 1981 $1.50

FILM/FOLK MUSIC   FEELIES/FRED FRITH
FLORIDA & FAR-AWAY/ALY IN LUCIER/FRANK FLOYD/FANZINES

Op

The "E" Op in two sections. Spring 1981 $1.50

INDEPENDENT
MUSIC

HARRY 'SWEETS' EDISON/CHARLES AMIRKHANIAN / EREBUS/EUTERPE
BILL EVANS / ROKY ERICKSON / EVERYTHING

eleven

9   95

elephants

ZIMB

According to some accounts, golden-era cassette culture grew out of the post-punk movement, with bands like Throbbing Gristle in the UK and The Residents in the US distributing music to fans via tape (one of Throbbing Gristle's most notorious releases was a brief-case containing 24 live cassettes, each one dubbed over an Abba album). In 1980, Bow Wow Wow, a British group managed by Malcolm McLaren, released the single 'C30 C60 C90 Go!', named for the different lengths of recordable cassette you could buy. They left the B-side blank so that fans could record their own music onto it. EMI dropped them shortly after.

KILLING RECORD INDUSTRY PROFITS

Blank tapes enabled an explosion of the musical bootleg. Named after illegally brewed Prohibition-era whisky, a bootleg is an illegally recorded piece of music, typically a recording of a live show. Both recording and distribution were made possible only thanks to tape. A whole scene of bootleggers grew up centred around, but not limited to, bands and musicians who toured and recorded prolifically, like Dylan or the Grateful Dead: "The simple fact is, if you don't have at least eleven versions of 'China Cat Sunflower/I Know You Rider' you're not really a die-hard Dead tape collector."[14]

The bootleg scene flourished on both sides of the Atlantic for decades, as documented in Clinton Heylin's absorbing *Bootleg! The Rise and Fall of the Secret Recording Industry* (2010). In London, Camden Market was an epicentre of the trade, thanks in part to the ministrations of a certain Big Al, who would stand in front of the speaker stack at gigs, recording them with a Walkman D6C. "He had farms of tape dubbing equipment, expensive industrial-strength machines", one fan recalls on a forum dedicated to The Smiths bootlegs. "If a Springsteen show finished at 23:00 Friday night, Al could and would have 100 copies of it on sale the next morning in Camden and on Portobello Road, complete with his trademark photocopied fluorescent inlays sporting an accurate track listing."[15] Then, in 1987, his stalls were raided by the police and Big Al disappeared forever (during the raid he was in Rotterdam taping a Bowie show, so presumably he simply stayed on in the Netherlands).

German-language cassette course, one example of the many non-musical uses of the medium.

The cassette always went hand-in-hand with unauthorised copying, sharing and distributing. For generations, making home-made tape recordings constituted many people's first act of criminal subversion. A fascinating 1979 article from sector organ *Billboard* details one California lawmaker's attempt to impose a 5 per cent surcharge on blank tapes, supposedly to recuperate losses occasioned by illegal copying. In opposition to this bill, however, one spokesman for the blank tape industry is quoted as saying that more than 50 per cent, and perhaps as many as 75 per cent, of blank tapes were put to non-musical uses, such as "education, religion and industrial training".[16]
One wonders if this estimate holds true throughout the history of the blank cassette (in other words, whether the most visible, iconic use of the blank tape – to record music quasi-illegally – in fact accounted for only a portion of the various applications it was put to). In any case, it seems that this bill was blocked, and a landmark US court ruling in 1984 finally upheld a consumer's right to copy music for their own personal use.

This didn't stop the industry pushing back. 'Home Taping Is Killing Music' was a slogan used by the British Phonographic Industry (BPI) to tie together a campaign they launched in the 1980s, when the rise of the bootleg had begun to seriously dent record sales. Universally reviled, the campaign had little effect. In fact, its most lasting impact was to give a movement a slogan, as when the Dead Kennedys (channelling Bow Wow Wow?) released a tape EP with one blank side, labelled: "Home taping is killing record industry profits! We left this side blank so you can help."

The back of the case of Dead Kennedys' *In God We Trust, Inc.*

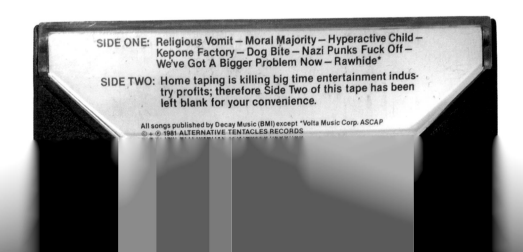

SIDE ONE: Religious Vomit — Moral Majority — Hyperactive Child — Kepone Factory — Dog Bite — Nazi Punks Fuck Off — We've Got A Bigger Problem Now — Rawhide*

SIDE TWO: Home taping is killing big time entertainment industry profits; therefore Side Two of this tape has been left blank for your convenience.

All songs published by Decay Music (BMI) except *Volta Music Corp. ASCAP
© + ℗ 1981 ALTERNATIVE TENTACLES RECORDS

Left:
Vinyl inlay printed with an
anti-home-taping slogan.

The bootleg was also to prove foundational in hip-hop culture. As Jeff Chang explains in *Can't Stop Won't Stop: A History of the Hip-Hop Generation* (2011), "Live bootleg cassette tapes of Kool Herc, Afrika Bambaataa, Flash and Furious 5, the L Brothers, the Cold Crush Brothers and others were the sound of the OJ Cabs that took folks across the city. The tapes passed hand-to-hand in the Black and Latino neighborhoods of Brooklyn, the Lower East Side, Queens and Long Island's Black Belt".[17] Grandmaster Flash would even charge uptown fans a dollar a minute for customised party tapes, periodically shouting out the buyer's name on the recording.

Early hip-hop was indivisible from the cassette. In fact, there is an argument that the musical form itself arose out of the creative possibilities opened up by tape technology. As Hebdige puts it in *Cut 'n' Mix*, "hip-hoppers 'stole' music off the air and cut it up. Then they broke it

down into its component parts and remixed it on tape. By doing that they were breaking the law of copyright. But the cut 'n' mix attitude was that no one owns a rhythm or sound. You just borrow it, use it, and give it back to the people in a slightly different form".

A POINTED ACT OF RESISTANCE

It is important to note that tape culture was far from a purely US or European phenomenon, as evidenced by studies such as Flagg Miller's book *The Moral Resonance of Arab Media: Audiocassette Poetry and Culture in Yemen* (2007) or the ethnographic essays 'Cassettes in culture: Emotion, politics, and performance in rural Tamil Nadu' (1995) by Paul David Greene, or 'Crafting Love: Letters and Cassette Tapes in Transnational Filipino Family Communication' (2011) by Mirca Madianou and Daniel Miller. Record label Sublime Frequencies' extensive catalogue is drawn in part from cassette cultures from around the world, with albums like *Cambodian Cassette Archives* and *Choubi Choubi! Folk and Pop Sounds from Iraq.*

Below:
Shagha Ariannia,
Our Future Is The Approaching Past,
2012, audio, cassette tape, recordings from 1978–1993 (Iranian Revolutionary Songs – family recordings), 20 minutes of audio, looped three times, courtesy of the artist

INDEX ٧٥ ,٩ ,٣ قىمتشرفت ردكترخ آرىن آرادىك سيد ـ ١

A
JAPAN

SONY.
TYPE I (NORMAL) POSITION   ➡   Compact Cassette   CHF60

The display of cassettes in a shop in Gamarra, a neighbourhood in Lima, Peru in December, 2018. Many collective vans, the backbone of the transport system, still feature cassette players. *Photo by Cristobal Pereira.*

The definitive history remains to be written of the audio cassette as a tool for political change. Long before the days of the so-called Twitter Revolution, Iranian exiles in Paris were recording incendiary cassettes that were smuggled back into Iran and played an important role in fomenting the 1979 revolution. As none other than Michel Foucault noted at the time, "If the Shah is about to fall, it will be due largely to the cassette tape. It is the tool *par excellence* of counter-information".[18]

Similarly, in the '70s and '80s cassette tapes were an important samizdat medium in the Soviet bloc. Poland was a hotbed of subversive taping, with fans recording over officially sanctioned releases and language-learning cassettes – "a practical necessity when blank tapes were hard to buy, but also a pointed act of resistance".[19] Czechoslovakian group Plastic People of the Universe, meanwhile, were imprisoned for their music in 1976, but were able to go on covertly recording and disseminating via tape.

MORE THAN JUST A FORMAT

As these scattered examples suggest, the cassette was much more than just a format. The USA-orientated cassette culture movement was the most visible and vocal manifestation of a radical shift in how media worked, towards a more open, hybrid, collective and participatory mode. The original proponents of cassette culture were pioneering a radical new vision of life as well as music. The self-sustaining, open-ended networks, the infinite profusion and variety of tastes, the melding of consumer and producer, the disregard for questions of copyright and legality – all these are approaches that have since come to predominate in the mainstream as well as at the margins.

It is significant that the logo of the 'Home Taping Is Killing Music' campaign, a nifty cassette-and-crossbones, lives on in the insignia of the Pirate Bay, the world's biggest file-sharing site, symbolic of the lineage that stretches from the first cassette culture bootleggers to today's digital buccaneers.

The Pirate Bay

Founder of Sound of Pig – "the pre-eminent cassette label of the heyday of cassette culture" – and later of Pogus Productions, Al Margolis is a prominent and renowned figure in the world of tapes. He is also a prolific maker of 'experimental' music, recording and touring as If, Bwana.

THE EDGE OF SOUND

Al Margolis, illustration by
Vincenzo Suscetta.

I first heard mention of independent cassettes in *OP* magazine, around 1980, '81. They had a very short cassette review column. So I started writing to people from there and connecting with the alternative culture of zines and cassettes. I found people who were doing stuff: Ladd-Frith (Psyclones), Viscera (Hal Mc-Gee and Debbie Jaffe), Chainsaw Tapes, and zines like *Cause and Effect*, *Objekt*, *Factsheet Five*, to name just a small sample. I started buying cassettes from people and just found weird stuff. Just kind of followed that path. This was pre-internet, so you would write to people: I read about you, heard your material on this cassette, do you have more. And it kind of went from there.

I had been doing a rock project called Pigs on Parade, but at one point I ended up buying a couple of synthesisers, a drum machine and a 4-track cassette. I still have it here, still works. I started recording myself, and that's where If, Bwana started. The idea for the cassette label basically came from: if I had my own label I could trade cassettes and not have to spend money. Sound of Pig Music was the name. In the beginning was a bunch of compilations, as well as single artists: Minoy, Zan Hoffman, Psyclones, Jim O'Rourke, there was a Merzbow/

John Hudak collaboration, a Dog as Master/If, Bwana collaboration. In the early days the music was – I don't want to say that in the end it got more specialised – but the early comps had punk stuff, weird folk things, experimental, people who couldn't play, some techno stuff. Then over time, as my own musical interests changed, it got a little more focused in there, more industrial. Noisy, if you want.

There just seemed to be a lot of interesting things starting. This was still pretty early in the process. Everybody was running labels; it was a family thing, you met a lot people. When I did some touring it was mostly through cassette people, I'd go out to places and see people I knew from the cassette scene. There was this underground. There was all kinds of stuff, both US and international artists. I was in touch with England, Germany, Japan, the Netherlands, Italy, some of the Scandinavian countries, Spain. Towards the end there was some stuff coming in from Brazil, Canada, Israel. Some stuff from behind the Iron Curtain. It was mostly Europe and Japan, but it was relatively international, considering.

Sound of Pig started in '84 and ran to about '89, '90. I did 301 cassettes during that time. Pogus, which started as an LP label, started about '88, so they kind of ran together for a year or two. That's when CDs were starting to come in and no one was producing LPs. Funny how things change. So for a while there was nothing going on. Everyone who was doing the cassette thing in the late '80s sort of disappeared. All the zines disappeared. I guess life intruded. People at radio stations weren't playing stuff – they always hated cassettes anyway, most of them. Interest levels kind of dropped away, it seemed like.

In terms of editions, I would do as many as I would do. I would just dub endlessly. I had a job as a shipping clerk for many years. I was by myself in the back office and I had three dubbing decks back there, so in the course of a work day I could dub 15, 20 tapes. And I had three or four dubbing decks at home. I could be doing four or five different tapes at a time. You'd make some artist's copies, probably about ten, then there was a number of people you'd send it to: magazines, zines, radio. So it was probably at least 50 of any edition. Maybe more. I still have a complete set, and most of the masters, too, gathering dust.

Back then, in the heyday, I was getting at least a tape or two every day in the mail. The great thing about the zines and compilations, there were always the contact addresses in there. I could dig out my old OPs and Sound Choices, there are little check marks, stars, question marks next to names – "Oh, this person sounds interesting". I'd write to most of those people, maybe get something in return. I mean, that's how we dealt with each other. There was a community. It really was this slow-moving process. You get something in the mail, it comes to you in three days, a week, a couple of weeks. It was a different pace.

It was pretty all encompassing. It was pretty much my life. Sound of Pig never made any money, it was a labour of love. And being a musician as well. Sundays was my recording day for If, Bwana stuff, I would just go into my little studio and do work. That's what I did. My wife was very supportive. That's what I did. I dubbed tapes. Every day, mail would come in, letters, cassettes, orders, every day I'd be mailing seven or eight packages. I'd be scouring the magazines. And then I'd be listening to stuff. Between '84 and '90, that's what I listened to. If you weren't willing to trade, I wouldn't bother, I really wasn't buying anything, I stayed out of the stores.

I've pretty much kept them all. I have thousands of cassettes. Cassettes and cassettes and cassettes. I signed a sort of agreement with the New York University library to give them most of my archives, cassettes and other stuff. More and more, I'm getting people asking questions. People interested in this stuff will be able to go into NYU and check it out. It's probably a decent place to be. I don't want to give it away to someplace no one will have access to, and I don't want to just sell it to somebody.

When this cassette revival first started, I've got to admit I was a little puzzled. When we were doing it, people not involved in the scene hated cassettes. We did it because it was cheap and it was easy. It was a communication device, you could reach people one-to-one. In fact, there have been multiple versions of cassette culture networks over the years. I remember Gen Ken Montgomery talking about going to Buffalo in the late '90s, and he met someone who was doing stuff about cassettes, and she knew nothing about the shit in the '80s, and he didn't know anyone she was talking about. So over the years it's kind of bounced around anyway. When the current scene started up again I was puzzled, but obviously it's the same thing. I mean, it's the same thing in the sense that it is the easiest and cheapest way to get your music around if you want something physical, and can't afford vinyl. But there is more of a choice these days – back then, CDs didn't exist. Part of it is a little bit the fetish of having something that's tangible, the collector's item aspect of it. And then you get the people who are like, "I only listen to cassette, I love the sound of cassette". Come on. Cassettes suck. No, I love cassettes, they have their charm, if you really want that grungy cassette sound. Where is the signal to noise ratio? Was that something he played, or was that just something on the cassette?

It's good that people making cassettes are actually getting back into the history. I used to go to independent record stores, and any book that mentioned cassettes at all talked about Merzbow, Jim O'Rourke, you know, four people. Or they mentioned Thurston Moore, who had nothing to fucking do with the cassette scene at that time. The fact that people have much more of a grasp of history, where it came from, and appreciate the vastness of it, how many people were involved, how long it's been going on, it's nice to actually have that happening.

My music goes on. If, Bwana is my own project which has continued over the years. I put my stuff out on Bandcamp now. I don't have to make anything physical. It's just there, you know. Pay me for it or not. Listen or not. That's sort of where I feel things are these days. People don't give a shit. Or there's too much to give a shit about. When you had to pay money, and wait for something in the mail, it actually had value. You anxiously waited for something to come: where's my cassette, I ordered it last week!

Mainly the stuff I've been doing lately is really quiet. I live out of the city, been here for almost 20 years. Maybe it's just years of listening to the woods. This tour I just went on, almost all the sets were acoustic. I was playing violin and clarinet as objects. So kind of quiet. A lot of the stuff I've been doing is almost like breathing. The space in between sounds, maybe? The space between notes. Almost trying to not play. I got a joke, if you actually hear a note it means I've screwed up. It's just sort of making people listen, focus in. Myself, too. So there's almost no sound. Which is really intense, actually. Doing that with the violin is interesting, because you can't hear anything if you're talking. You hear people's attention being sucked in. The edge of sound, how about that. I'm trying to reach the edge of sound.

R. Stevie Moore was born in Nashville in 1952. In 1982, he set up the R. Stevie Moore Cassette Club to distribute his own releases, which he has been doing ever since. To date he has released around 300 albums. As a pioneer of so-called lo-fi music and one of the most prominent figures in the original cassette underground, he is often referred to as the godfather of home recording, an epithet he only grudgingly accepts.

I TRY NOT TO BE NEGATIVE ABOUT THE CASSETTE THING

It's about the music. Cassettes were just a certain avenue, way back then. I was doing reel-to-reel tapes before cassettes in the '70s, which is when my whole career started to flower. The DIY thing. I was already doing that for ten years before suddenly there was this new format, and it was perfect for me. I just jumped in and took advantage of it.

I left Nashville in 1978 right as Punk and New Wave started happening, and suddenly my career started taking off, in a tiny way. I just fell into it. I don't recall there being a movement. Although I wasn't the only one, naturally. The convenience of it was wonderful. The best thing about tape was that it was so easy to mail via the postal system. That was the best thing, the size of it. And the fidelity was great. In retrospect, I had no problem with the fidelity. And that's ironic, because they constantly call me the king of lo-fi. I can live with it but I hate it, because it has nothing to do with fidelity. Cassette was just perfect for our junk finances.

Back then there was no other real option. We didn't really need another option. Vinyl was always the dream, but that was out of

R. Stevie Moore, illustration by Luca Bendandi.

the question for people who couldn't afford it. It was the beginning of, hey, make your own records at home. You don't need a middleman, you don't have to ask someone to decide if it's good music, or if it's a good sequence, and for me that was perfect because my whole thing has been not only being prolific but releasing everything I've done. Without having to ask somebody. And of course it's artistic suicide, because there's way too much for people to discover. They have to wade through hundreds and hundreds of songs. And I can live with that, too.

I've always been proud that my main thing, besides being prolific and releasing everything and not even editing at all, is that the styles of my music are diverse. So cassettes were perfect for me long before people even did mixtapes. My own music was a mixtape because I do all different styles. I was really brought up on free-form radio, you know, soft and then loud and then good and then bad and then fast and then slow. Variety is my main thing. And that's something that not many people in the cassette revolution were doing. They were either indie bands, indie rock, or industrial or folk or country and only that. So not only was the cassette perfect for me, it was perfect to make my diversity heard. And I had a blast in putting together my own music because of the cassette phenomenon. I'd reach the end of Side A and then start Side B, and my own home-made music was done that way as well. I didn't put together 15, 20 songs and then resequence them and try to figure out which ones would flow best on this cassette. It wasn't like that at all. I was doing it before cassettes, with tape decks, bouncing it back and forth, ruining the quality. Some of these things had up to ten overdubs. But I never went back to repair them or remix them or rethink them. I'd move on to the next song.

But back in the day there wasn't so much influence in terms of people doing DIY or mixtapes. That came later. I never had a real label so it wasn't like I was seeking other bands or artists to release. There was no need to and I wouldn't have been able to do that anyway because my main artist, R. Stevie Moore, was already too much to deal with. In the mid-'80s I was putting out 15 albums a year. Because I was just recording that much. And it didn't matter if that was too much. There was nobody that was going to tell me, hey, you're recording too much. How ridiculous is that? I couldn't control it, and I didn't want to control it.

But trying to stay specific with the tape concept itself. I really appreciate and respect all the attention that the cassette tape is getting today, but I also scratch my head in bewilderment, because I really don't know what that has to do with anything. I don't even have a player now. People continue wanting to send me their cassettes and it's just a waste. Like, send me a zip file. In some ways I never thought I would say that. Am I being unfaithful to my roots? Well, of course I am. Because the world has progressed. I try not to be negative about the cassette thing. But I have every reason to be. Because I'm such an old man, I've been through it all, and it really doesn't apply to right now.

And yet there are cassette labels that approach me who want to put something out and I'll say, hell yeah. Let's do something. Send me 20 copies and then we're finished with it. There's no money. It's very romantic for me, very nostalgic, to think back to when I was cutting out j-cards and buying cases of TDK C90s. So, you know, it's strange. There's no way the kids who worship this cassette thing can understand how it is for me. And there's no way I can understand how it is for them, I guess.

I'm pretty much retired from making music.

As far as writing pop/rock, I haven't done that in a while, I miss it, but I have health issues and my main job is just maintaining the enormous catalogue of R. Stevie Moore. I'm on the internet constantly, I hate it. I'm just trying to continually get people interested in my music and buy my records. My main music-making these days is mixology, turntablism, mashups, that kind of thing. And also spoken word. I've given up, I've written 40,000 pop/rock songs and I'm kind of fed up with the effort of doing that. Now I just turn the mic on and speak. I have a great radio voice.

There's no way to feel sad about moving from tapes to CDs. That's the next chapter that happened to me. I worshipped CDRs when that happened. Never did I get sad. Because suddenly, now you didn't have to worry about tape and you could actually press your own records on the CDRs, at home. I even had CD burners. Before computers and disc drives and that whole thing, I actually went through four or five professional CD burners. And that was fantastic. It was better than tape. And I continue to champion CDs. Now that so many people are saying CD is over. Even my car doesn't have a CD player. I love CDs.

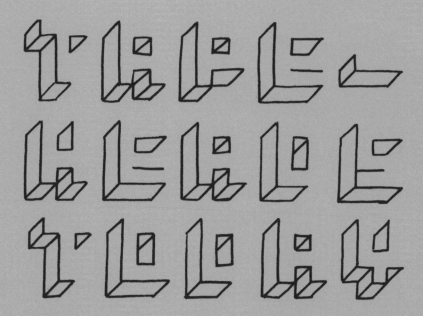

According to Robin James, the original cassette underground's most prominent chronicler, today's tape culture is only "an esoteric and eccentric historical folk art, some kind of anachronistic re-enactment club".[20] In one sense he is right, but in many others he is not.

Recall that, first time round, the materiality of the cassette was a secondary consideration – tape was simply the only option available for recording music cheaply. So while bootleggers, experimental musicians and hip-hop DJs all spent hours fiddling with scraps of tape, there wasn't really a feeling that they were bound together by the format, any more than different musicians are bound together by the fact they use YouTube. It was a means, not an end.

National Audio Company in Springfield, Missouri, USA. A detail of the slitting room machinery: master rolls of coated and polished tape are slit into narrow spools approximately 4 millimetres wide for use in cassette tapes.

Today, by contrast, every single person who records tapes makes the conscious decision to focus on this platform, with all it entails. Tape is no longer the cheapest and easiest way to put music out, and rather than connect you to a wide range of people, it in fact closes you off: who even owns a tape player? It is this wilful, quixotic immersion in the past that James labels eccentric.

But to dismiss contemporary cassette culture as reactionary revivalism or retro fetishism is to miss the point entirely. Cassette culture today is not (just) about rebooting a technology that has nominally been surpassed. To see things in the right light, we need to trace what lies behind the surge in popularity the format is currently experiencing.

To be sure, a few diehard tape lovers never even noticed the CD had been and gone. America's biggest tape manufacturer, National Audio Company, hardly missed a beat in terms of production, even if for the last 20 years its clients have mostly been religious groups and kindergartens. But only a few years ago even the diehards would never have dreamed that cassette sales were going to increase by over 100% in 2018.

To be clear, tapes are not going to redefine the musical panorama any time soon. Despite that surge, cassettes only accounted for a trifling quantity of all album sales, and most of those were of a specific kind of knowingly nostalgic product: *Guardians of the Galaxy*-related albums were big sellers, as was the *Stranger Things* soundtrack, a release that milks the retro-tech touch for all it's worth.

So it is not about sales volumes. To catch the tape in its natural habitat, in the context where it makes most sense, we need to shift focus away from the music-buying mainstream, to the bleeding edge of experimentation, mutant sounds never even considered for mass production: music too weird to live, too rare to die.

The thunder wall, ice sounds, chattering, electro-cheeze, messy, yowling, droning and punctuated chanting, surprisingly orchestrated, reggae ghost-dancing, electronic ringing and glowing, outerspace flotsam and satellites, voices and guitar collages, sweet singing with guitar, vocals a bit twangy, homemade heavy metal shouted in English with thick German accents, tumbling electronics, studio magic rock, earnest nice guy vocals, au

naturel people singing in a group in the field, sappy pop crap with expressive vocalists, muddled rock with rhythm boxes, odd collages of classic choral singing, electro-mechanical chattering, spunky homemade humor rock, revolutionary tribal noise-chunks, beautiful electronic landscaping, boating in a pond with friends, scientifically mixed collage samples, pounding heavy rock with a hamburger-throated singer, celestial tinkling, soaring keyboard wings, the sound of a London subway with strange electronic visitors, any imaginable instrument imitated electronically (bells for example), dramatic poetry with odd sound effects in the background, wailing electric guitars crunching and screaming, plastic angel choirs menaced by ocean liners, electronic devices fashioning their own escape devices, a live show in an English bar with a bar-fight between songs, glossy instrumental music suitable for banks, a crazy radio show with Sub-Genius influences, outright madness made with organs and microphones, unending synthesizer babbling, etc., etc.

Extract from *Cassette Mythos*, the first book to document cassette culture and the revolutionary potential of the tape.

The remarkable passage on the opposite page is from *Cassette Mythos* (1992), a seminal book-length zine about tapes edited by Robin James. It is an evocation of the pile of cassettes that James has on his desk, awaiting review. He was writing decades ago, but one suspects that a random sampling of music released on tape today would yield a not entirely dissimilar list. From grindcore to vaporwave, to power ambient to drone, those who want to keep an ear on the newest experimental sounds are increasingly doing it through cassette, or at least MP3 versions of cassette releases. Why?

MATERIALITY. CEREMONY. COST

One characteristic of the cassette that speaks to experimentally minded millennials is its very materiality. Music has become disassociated from physical reality. Many contemporary music lovers don't even bother downloading MP3s, preferring to live with their heads in the cloud. It is consequently an uncanny and pleasant feeling to be able to hold a piece of music in your hand. This materiality also helps to recapture a sense of the ritual which used to precede listening to music. Opening the case, glancing at the cover, choosing the right side, pressing eject, hitting play... Perhaps older generations weren't aware of it (seeing it as an unavoidable mechanical fact), but this elaborate process helps to clear and focus the mind.

Today, most aspects of our existences are mediated by a screen. Much of what we do on a day-to-day basis, from ordering food to finding a sexual partner to monitoring our bodily well-being, involves a limited range of minute variations on the same minimal physical gesture, executed with a forefinger. In this context, the simple act of putting on a tape involves stepping outside of daily life, acceding to a ceremonial state, priming yourself for sonic revelation.

Kylie Minogue recently released a tape version of her *GOLDEN* album, and the video she made to promote it perfectly exemplifies our central thesis here. Watch how she opens the case and even sniffs the fresh cassette, in raptures about its physicality, then exclaims "Oh, the sound of it!", as she slips it into the device.

Another thing that's different about tapes is that it is hard to skip tracks. But what was once one of the limitations of the format – that you can't home in on individual songs without a certain amount of to-ing and fro-ing – has today become a boon. Putting on a tape, one tends to let it play till it stops, and then flip it round. As with an LP, listening to only one side of a tape can feel like eating half a meal, as it should. You are therefore immersed in a tape for much longer than you tend to be immersed in a digital format. The fact you can't check your emails on a hi-fi probably also makes it easier to put on a tape and leave it on. You are less likely to pause a tape to watch a video, then forget to press play again and sit in silence for 20 minutes before you even notice, trashing your experience of the music.

Related to this is the fact that, knowing a significant portion of the evening will be dedicated to each tape, you can sometimes find yourself carefully lining up three or four cassettes to listen to in a certain order. This approach to consuming music is very far from passive: arranging albums in a narrative arc, curating an ambience. This feels like a very obvious thing to do with tapes or LPs, but it is hard to replicate the feeling with MP3s. And even if you do plan to listen to a sequence of albums on the computer, shuffling round tapes and making a little stack of the ones you want to hear is phenomenologically far richer a process than cuing up iTunes.

In short, one might feel that producers and consumers of tape music count on a more extensive engagement than that encouraged by most streaming interfaces. As a listener, it is refreshing to be invited simply to sit and focus. In the words of Rinus van Alebeek, tapes "all

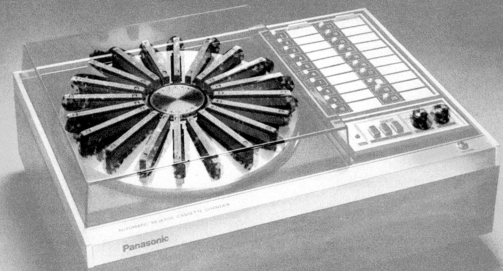

move at the same speed, 176.4 metres an hour, a very peaceful pace which gives you the time to observe things in a different way". Sinister corporations with nonsensical names have conspired to decimate your attention span. Cassettes work to undo that damage.

It is also possible to enjoy the therapeutic materiality of the cassette without even engaging with the music on it. Indeed, it seems probable that many of the people who buy a tape at a merch stall don't own a tape player, and simply cannot listen to it. But in its new incarnation reproducing music is just one of the cassette's roles. Tapes these days almost always come with a download code for the music they contain. The MP3s often won't have been redubbed back onto the computer, as it were, so the sonic quality of the format is irrelevant. And a cassette's cover and liner notes often act as an outlet for a band or label's aesthetic vision, allowing for a more personalised approach to branding that both complements and enhances the music. So the cassette becomes a beautiful souvenir and a personal, hand-to-hand way to share digital music. For fans it is a chance to cherish something physical, something which often still bears the mark of its maker – an unmistakably human artefact.

And finally, there is the cost aspect. If you want to sponsor a physical release for any one of the reasons sketched above, tape is a low-cost and high-ish fidelity alternative to vinyl. For a handful of currency units you can put out an album in a week. An aspect of this is the elision of consumer and producer, so typical of cassette cultures through the years. Talking to contemporary tape labels, a sense emerges of how the whole operation can be collective.

The negligible cost of the process means that non- or anti-commercial communities, grassroots economies of exchange, thrive around the cassette, oblivious to profit margins. In fact, tape today, like tape yesterday, is as much about the networks it helps build as the music it contains.

CASSETTE STORE
DAY USA 2018

www.cassettestoredayusa.com

U READY?

CSD HAPPENS SATURDAY, OCTOBER 13, 2018

Consider the LP. Record sales – as in, sales of actual records – have increased in the US for 12 years straight; in the first half of 2018, 7.6 million were sold, a year-on-year increase of 19.2 per cent. This is a heartening figure for lovers of physical formats, but it is also a misleading one in some ways. The majority of these sales are of albums that were released more than 30 years ago, and in fact most of them are classics in the vein of *Sgt. Pepper's Lonely Hearts Club Band*. This suggests that many of the people buying vinyl are doing so not out of a love of contemporary music, but in order to recapture the essence of their youthful listening. Indeed, a couple of years ago UK-based research firm YouGov published a report which suggests that older generations are indeed largely responsible for vinyl's comeback. "When compared to the adult population as a whole, those that have purchased a vinyl album recently are more likely to be aged between 45-54. By contrast, those in the 18-24 age group are the least likely."[21] The same report also observes that vinyl buyers are more likely to "enjoy being alone".

In other words, the much-trumpeted resurgence of record sales is more a moment than a movement. It isn't really about a community, except by default, and there is not much that's contemporary to it.

The opposite is true of tapes. As much as music, cassette culture today seems to be premised on building networks and sharing experiences.

A key reference point is Cassette Store Day, a worldwide celebration of the tape. Created in the UK in 2013, by 2016 it had come to feature shops in the US, Australia, New Zealand, Germany, France, and Japan, and the initiative is now run on an international scale, managed collaboratively by Blak Hand Records (UK), Burger Records (USA) and VSI (Japan).

Burger Records are behind the organisation of Cassette Store Day.

Cassette Store Day is just one of a whole range of tape-oriented events that take place around the world. In Berlin, the Tape Summit is into its third installment. This festival of cassette labels is run by the team at Tape Dub, a Berlin-based company that duplicates cassettes for a range of independent labels and bands. According to head honcho Sara Valentino, the success of the Tape Summit came from the number and variety of collaborations the events have sparked.

Tape Dub itself has an interesting business model. They produce short runs of releases, from 20 up to 1,000. The label sends them the file or CD or master tape, and they copy the tapes as well as printing the graphic material and sourcing the case. Their turnaround varies from one week to several, depending on the size of the order and whether they have the tapes in stock. With their relatively high-end Sony equipment, they can record up to seven tapes simultaneously, and make thousands of copies a month.

The example of Tape Dub suggests how different types of tape-based organisations can become focal nodes of a community, dedicated equally to developing a sustainable business model and building connections.

Another example of an organisation that plays this role is Waltz, the Tokyo cassette store. Set up in August 2015, it has already acquired global renown. Aside from having been named a 'Gucci place' by the fashion brand, Waltz has fostered links with tape organisations all over the world, and an offline community has grown up around the store itself. Tellingly, perhaps, founder Taro Tsunoda worked for 14 years at Amazon Japan before opening the store, which boasts an inventory of more than 6,000 tapes.

These are just a few examples of the type of organisation and event that are increasingly growing up around the contemporary cassette scene. As the format's prominence grows, the networks they enable will only spread further and grow stronger.

So, to return to Robin James for the third and final time, today's tape scene may well be esoteric, and it is certainly eccentric, but it is not historical. There was never any rupture in cassette culture, it just went further underground. Around the world today, people are doing what they have always done with tapes. Turn your back on the mainstream, focus on a format that will at best cover your costs, and spend your weekends in the company of people guaranteed to be on a level, people who, like you, only want to record, release, and listen to exciting new music: choose tape!

The following pages feature a selection of releases from tape labels around the world, as well as texts compiled from interviews with their founders.

Right:
Waltz Tokyo, an image of the shopfront.

Below:
Cassette players and boomboxes on sale at the shop. *Images courtesy of Waltz Tokyo.*

"Hey, we're not trying to be different and cool by releasing music on a tape, let's make that clear. At one point, it was our only option. It was ride or die. And now, it has stuck. People know Blak Hand as a cassette label, which we dig. We don't sign the bands, we work on a project with them and let them feel free to come to us with their ideas and it just works. No broken hearts. We believe that a hard-working band deserves to get their music heard. At Blak Hand, we want to be the stepping stone for bands, a home where they can begin their journey, express themselves without judgement and take something physical to the major labels one day to say, 'look, this is what we can do'. Hopefully by releasing cassettes, we extend the longevity of music in this digital age. Much like our parents showed us their record collections growing up, we may still be able to do the same." **Blak Hand Records, UK** *blakhandrecords.bandcamp.com*

"Field Hymns started in Portland, Oregon in 2010: about eight years and around 80 releases ago. Our philosophy is to not screw anyone over, to release artists and albums we enjoy (not just artists that could be financially successful, though the temptation is there), and to try like mad to get people to listen to our albums. I'd say we've been successful so far, as we break even, and that is really the best one can hope for. We may lose money on your release, but dammit, it will look good and we will fight for it. I can only hope that mantra is at the core of every label's heart." **Field Hymns Records, USA** *fieldhymns.com*

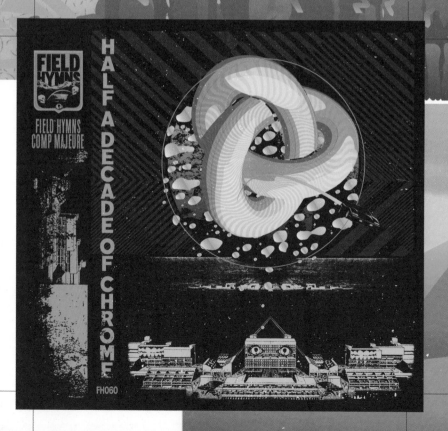

"Umor Rex is oriented to sound and the visual aesthetic. I love international architecture from the middle of the last century, Soviet propaganda, Swiss typography, German design, and post-revolutionary Mexican statements. All these concepts are very abstract in relation to music but, I don't know why or how, they are always ingredients in the music we release. It is music played electronically, with interfaces, and synthetic sounds deliberately manipulated by the human being. Umor Rex is not exclusively a cassette label, but yes, a big part of our catalogue is on tape. I need physical and tangible objects. I love the cassette, and it allows us to have more continuity, as well as exploring more artists and sounds." **Umor Rex, Mexico** *umor-rex.org*

BRETT NAUCKE

EXECUTABLE DREAMTIME

UMOR REX RECORDS UR091

SIAVASH AMINI & MATT FINNEY

UMOR REX RECORDS

SR HESS + RM ZUYDERVELT — RE-COLLECTING

M.GEDDES GENGRAS — TWO VARIATIONS (2015)

SHAPES — MELFI — SPLIT

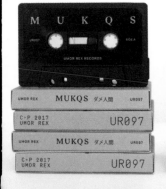

MUKQS

UMOR REX RECORDS

MUKQS

ダメ人間

UMOR REX RECORDS UR097

THÉ DÉLUGE

UMOR REX RECORDS

THÉ DÉLUGE

FOREST STRUCTURES

UMOR REX RECORDS UR098

"Our philosophy has been clear from the get-go. We want to release music that we can sleep to, drive to, eat to, live to... Atmospheric and grounded in nature are usually the sounds we look for in Bastakiya Tapes releases. Some of the advantages of tape are cheaper production, warm analogue sounds and a tangible music format. The visual aspects are personal moments captured through various types of cameras, and the story embedded through the music." **Bastakiya Tapes, United Arab Emirates** *bastakiyatapes.bandcamp.com*

"In 2018 we celebrated the label's 20th anniversary. Our first cassette releases were in 2004 though, launched with a subscription series called the Deathbomb Arc Tape Club. Subscribers were sent a new tape every month for a year, and each one had a single 10 minute song on each side from a different artist. Our credo is 'Genres Unknown'. We just want each new artist we work with to be unlike anything we've ever heard before, including any other acts on the label. It always blew my mind that some of the bigger acts we've worked were down to do cassettes: No Age, Death Grips, clipping., Deerhoof. Probably the most memorable cassette release we've done is the DIALER cassette, confusingly entitled 'CDr', which had handmade shells." **Deathbomb Arc, USA** *deathbombarc.com*

"Not Not Fun began in February 2004. We owned a dual-cassette deck and therefore could duplicate as many (or as few) copies as we wanted. We also grew up with a fondness for the medium, having made mixtapes throughout our teenage years. We're currently up to catalogue number 344, spanning vinyl, tapes, CDs, and one art book. Our philosophy is to champion the overlooked, ignored, or unknown. Be true to your tastes. Cultivate enthusiasm. It's interesting how much appreciation of the cassette has grown across the past decade and a half. Streaming services and iPods and cloud-based developments will never fully replace the desire among some for a tangible object to collect or cherish. We are physical beings; it's not surprising some of us feel a unique connection to physical music." **Not Not Fun, USA** *notnotfun.com*

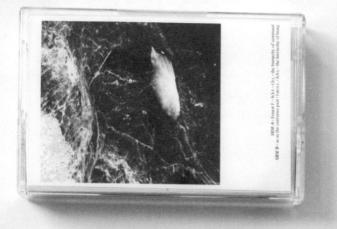

SIDE A - Ernest P - h.b.t - t.b.t - the hierarchy of command
SIDE B - as on the centuries past - t.m.o.c - h.b.t - the hierarchy of being

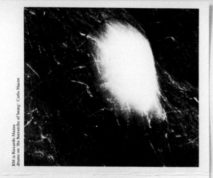

RM is Riccardo Mazza
drums on the hierarchy of being : Carlo Mascee

SIDE A - Ernest P - h.b.t - t.b.t - the hierarchy of command
SIDE B - as on the centuries past - t.m.o.c - h.b.t - the hierarchy of being

RM
THE HIERARCHY OF BEING

YEREVAN
TAPES
YER026

Redeem at yere

"Looking at our catalogue, one might notice differences rather than similarities between the artists, but they all share a common aim. Their search for subterranean sounds may end in different artistic solutions, but what moves them seems to be the same: a quest for spiritual inquiry. With regard to the tape format, cassette has been a natural medium for experimental music since the '70s, if not before. So it comes as no surprise that we felt it was our primal platform. It's cheap, it's easy to distribute worldwide, it gives you an opportunity to release material from obscure artists without having to face the challenges of vinyl record production. Plus, it's a great object which puts you in touch with memories of your childhood days, at least for those of us who were born in the '80s. It gives one that familiar feeling of holding something familiar in your hands, and at the same time it keeps a little magic within itself."

Yerevan Tapes, Italy *yerevantapes.com*

"We are not sure what future will bring, but we want Z Tapes to grow. The cassette movement will find a steady place in the music world, even if the hype dies down. I think there will be fewer articles about cassettes and more conventional press about releases on cassettes. Hopefully, major media can move beyond writing about the novelty of the medium and instead acknowledge it as a standard for album releases. I expect that more people will be supporting cassette labels and more great music will be released on this format in the coming years. I hope there will be more stores with a wide cassette selection, and that the fans of this medium will be found all over the world. One day, people will stop questioning why you are doing cassettes and simply be excited about it. Cassettes and music released on them will be an important part of music world. Hopefully, we will still be part of it, too!" **Z Tapes, Slovakia** *ztapesrecords.com*

"Our label was born in 2015 in Madrid. The idea was and is to put out little-known projects combining two things that we are passionate about: music and design. We believe that it is absolutely necessary that the music be accompanied by a defined image and graphic style. Make it a complete package, so it acquires greater meaning. The fact that major labels are increasingly making more cassette editions is something to think about. We believe there will always be a small space for this format that we love so much. ¡Larga vida al cassette!"
Solid Tapes, Spain *solidtapes.bandcamp.com*

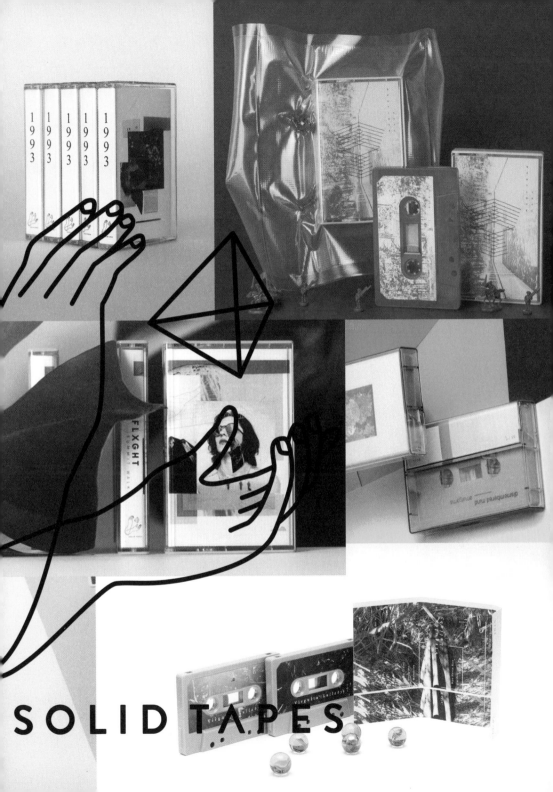

SOLID T.A.P.E.S

Image courtesy of Solid Tapes.

Burger Records was started by Sean Bohrman and Lee Rickard in Fullerton, California more than a decade ago. Since then, Burger has become a behemoth in independent music, as well as trailblazer and focal point for the worldwide 'cassette revival'.

We first started making tapes in 2007. We were on tour in Kansas City and I remember after the show we were sitting in the van listening to The GO. And it dawned on me that nobody was making tapes of any of these awesome records that were coming out at the time. So I got on the computer in the parking lot right there and I emailed The GO, Traditional Fools, which was Ty Segall's band at the time, and Apache, because those were the three albums we were listening to non-stop in the van. And I asked if they wanted to do tapes. And they all said yeah.

And then it just started to snowball. Now we've released over a thousand different titles on cassette. We've made probably over 500,000 cassettes over the last 11 years. We didn't plan

Burger Records
California, USA
burgerrecords.com

it or think it would take off like it did. But... it did! People started doing stories on us and we started getting in the *New York Times* and the *LA Times* and the *Wall Street Journal* and stuff. Everybody was doing this cassette revival story, and they're still doing it, we still get people doing that story.

I guess we're at the forefront of it, just because when we started doing it, people said this is stupid, this is dumb, why are you doing tapes again. Everybody was making fun of us, but we just kept doing it, doing it, doing it. When we first started we were working with Sub Pop and Vice and Universal and all of these record labels. They didn't see it as anything they wanted to do, and they were just like, sure. It was like a grey area, so it got our foot in the door for a lot of different bands and titles and stuff, that if we were looking to make a CD or an LP we would never have been able to do. Like, Weezer's management called us to do one of their albums on cassette. We made a thousand copies and sold them all in a weekend. And there was no contract, there was nothing. He just called us up and said, hey, you want to do this? And we were like, sure! Same thing with Green Day. We re-released *Dookie* on cassette for Cassette Store Day, and there was no contract. But now people see that you can make a dollar or two off of a cassette, so it's gotten a lot harder to collab with bigger labels. Because they're making their own cassettes now. But back when we started nobody was making cassettes, and they were laughing at us for making cassettes.

What is it about the cassette that first drew you to it as a format?

It's quick to make, it's cheap to make. It fits in your pocket. And if you master it well it'll sound good. You can make tapes for your friends. It's a personal thing. It's not like when you make a CD, you can burn ten CDs for ten people in ten

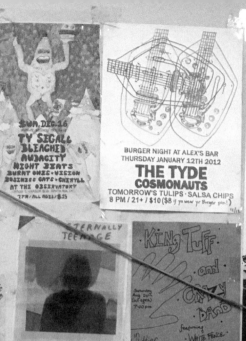

minutes, you know, so there's no love behind it. But when you make a mixtape for somebody, it's special, to make a tape for somebody you really have to sit there and create the tape, and it takes a long time. I think that in a world where we're constantly going towards the quick and the easy and the fast and the now, there's a select group of people who want love and handmade stuff and real things. Things that mean something and that aren't just disposable. Kids today grew up with CDs, they grew up doing the MP3 thing, and they're like, OK, I'm over this, now I want something else.

Do you think cassette revival is the right way to describe it?

That's what they call it, the cassette revival or whatever. But it's not a nostalgia thing, because a lot of the people who are buying these cassettes were born in the late '90s and weren't around for the boom of cassettes like we were. So, like I said, people want something physical in their hands, they don't want to listen to MP3. I mean, there's nothing special about an MP3. Anybody can make it, send it. But LPs, cassettes, there's something special about them. I think that's what people see in this format. And for bands, the turnaround is weeks as opposed to months when you're dealing with LPs. Right now, because there's a resurgence in vinyl as well, it's gotten a lot more expensive and a lot more time-consuming to make vinyl. So, in the face of that, being able to make cassettes in a couple of weeks, or even a couple of days, is invaluable. To have something on the table, to sell for bands on tour and things, makes sense in our world. It's not like we planned for this niche thing to blow up and for people to write books about it and stuff. But it is interesting. It is kind of confounding to think about this format that everybody thought was dead and gone coming back. The cassette was how we built our business, pretty much.

You guys have got a pretty big community now around the project, with Cassette Store Day, the store and your various events.

We do Burger Mania, Burger Rama, Burger Boogaloo, Burger Oasis... We do Burger Invasion shows, tons of shows all over the world, all year round.

And you have a good following?

Yes, we've been really blessed and lucky in that regard.

It seems like a lot of labels have popped up in the States in recent years.

For sure. I talk to so many people who are like, I started a record label because of you guys. Because to make a tape label you don't have to invest a ton of money, and everybody's got friends who are in bands, so it's really easy to start. Burger has inspired other people to start their own labels and do their own thing. Probably because they see us doing it and they're like, if these fools can make this happen, why can't I? It's been really cool. The reason we started the record label is to spread music and to inspire people. Definitely not to make money. Because, you know, we're making enough money to sustain ourselves, but that's about it. We're not rolling in cash or anything. But we are happy. And I like where the label's at and I like where my life is at. And that's success. That means we're successful. Success isn't a monetary thing. Happiness is the measure of success. So I think as long as we keep doing things that make us happy and not worry about what other people think or how other people perceive us or what we're doing, I think that's a measure of success. And as long as we can keep doing that and keep paying the bills, that's going to be our legacy. When we're dead, Burger Records will still be talked about and remembered. And that's what I wanted out of life, pretty much, to do something that builds a legacy for myself and my friends.

If you wanted to give a few words of advice to someone who wanted to start up their own tape label, what would they be?

Me, I'm a workaholic, obsessive compulsive. All I do is work on Burger. If you want to be successful at anything in life, you have to just put your blinders on and focus on what you want, on your dream, on how you want to achieve it. I don't go to parties, I've never been a party person. I don't drink really, I just smoke a lot of weed. If you want to be successful you just have to work really, really hard. And you have to miss out on some things because you're going to be working. Another good thing about Burger is that it never gets boring or repetitive or old, there's always something new happening. You don't really get to savour any victories or regret any losses because there's always something new happening, you can't dwell on stuff.

How are things going with the store?

We're having a grand re-opening tomorrow. We expanded into the shop next to us, we're twice as big. This is our best year ever for the shop and we've had some of our best months ever for the label this year. But the more you grow, the more you have to get wrapped up in the business side of things, contracts and stuff.

That's not why I got into the record business. I didn't even plan on getting into the record business, but that's not why I'm here, that's not what I enjoy doing.

When we started, I put in 100 bucks and Lee put in 100 bucks and then we released our first tape. And then we used the money from that tape to pay for the next tape and so on, until we were releasing 200 to 300 tapes a year. We're trying to slow down, but there's a lot of good music. We like turning people on to music and discovering new music. It overwhelms me, the amount of music that we put out. But that's what it's all about, discovering new music. If you want to run a successful record label, find bands that are already successful and release their music, you'll have a successful record label, it'll be awesome. But that's not fulfilling for me. I love finding a band nobody's heard of and then watching them grow and become really popular. That's what it's all about for me, that's what I love doing.

And you have to get your friends involved. You can't do it by yourself. I'm not a party person but Lee, the guy I started the record label with, he's a very sociable person and we have a yin-yang type thing going on. I like it that way, it works out. So you've got to find somebody you can work with, to help fill some of the gaps.

It's all about following through. Everything that we do – Weiner Records, all of our side projects – are all jokes that we had when we were driving somewhere, you know, and we took the joke too far and it became an LP and a business. That's what Burger was. It was a joke and became this big thing. Our whole lives.

Founded in 2017 with a name meaning 'the irresistible urge to dance', Nyege Nyege Tapes has quickly become one of East Africa's most dynamic outsider music projects. The label is just one aspect of an initiative bringing together a musical residency programme, a year-round calendar of cultural events, and an ever-growing music festival, held each year in an abandoned resort deep in the Ugandan jungle.

What does the music scene look like in Kampala?

The music scene in Kampala and East Africa is thriving. A lot of new sounds, a lot of new producers exploring new territories. More and more exposure of what other producers in the region are doing, and more conversations between disparate styles. Performance opportunities are also growing, as local electronic music is becoming more widely accepted by commercial promoters. A very young population combined with a general deep love for music, dance and partying, as well as increased access to laptops and internet, means more and more young people can get into production and teach themselves. Traditionally, the problem was a lack of exposure to other kinds of music both

Nyege Nyege Tapes
Kampala, Uganda
nyegenyegetapes.bandcamp.com

from inside Africa and the rest of the world, other than commercial US hip-hop and Jamaican dancehall and Naija pop, which in some ways was a hindrance to musical innovation.

Our label focuses on these little weird islands of creativity. Like Otim Alpha, who takes wedding songs from the Acholi Guru tribe in the north east and reinterprets them electronically. Or the Sounds of Sisso album, which sounds like Gabber but, I can tell you, these guys have never listened to techno in their lives. So musical isolation can also produce interesting results.

Does Nyege Nyege handle its own financing?

We fund almost everything ourselves. Before it was with our day jobs, and now slowly, slowly we have some support from commercial sponsors, and record sales and touring are providing meaningful incomes to a lot of the artists in our collective. The idea was always that the festival would become the income generator for all the other projects. It's going into its fifth edition now. It's been growing: it started with 1,500 in the first year, and this year we had 9,000 people. And we'll cap it at that for the time being, as we've lost a bit of control over the production aspects. This year there was international media there, Resident Advisor, FACT, Boiler Room, and with that comes... you know.

The club nights came first. Then we started the festival. Before the festival, though, we rented this big house and put up two community studios in there. There's space for between 10 and 15 artists to stay at any one time. So that runs the whole year and that's really become the pole through which a lot of the music comes out. We do residencies, both with people from outside Africa who we feel make sense, and art-

ists from around Africa. Primarily it's music, but we also do some film, installations, and now we want to explore things like publishing.

What are your criteria for deciding who to release?

Again, because of this ecosystem that we've built up, our relation to musicians comes about in very different ways. Through releases, or they can come for residences at our studio, they can stay there, sometimes we have a bit of kit to give an artist or some extra software. We run year-round production workshops. In general we are excited by music from here that plays with the usual expectations that people have of contemporary African music.

Generally, when people release with us, it is just one phase in our relationship. The relationship continues with trying to arrange shows, touring, helping artists get passports, not always a straightforward exercise here, and assisting in further musical projects and releases.

Who makes up the Nyege Nyege team? It seems like a very diverse crew.

It's a mix of various people. There's a whole team at the studio, a lot of young producers. Producers also come to get training and they end up staying, becoming part of the team. They start doing the events, so they do the local promotion. And we're sure a few of them in a few years' time will start their own labels. That'll be really fun, to see five or six little labels popping up in Kampala. The idea with the Sounds of Sisso guys is to help them start their own label. Because they're a recording studio now. But, for them, doing a label means putting out music to get shows, and putting out music in a way that'll help you get shows: you have to get it into the hands of the right people. But for us the aim of the label is a bit broader, for it to function as a space where you're curating a musical trajectory. In the sense of exploring certain streams or angle of musical styles that we find are relevant, that are expressing more than just dance, that encompass a punk and DIY approach.

How do people listen to music in Uganda?

There's a huge difference between the big cities and the rural areas; it's still primarily a rural country. But mobile phones are the main way people listen to music, via MP3s, which you swap via Bluetooth, or micro-SD cards.

You can buy a DVD with lots and lots of MP3s on it. Or you just go across the street, where you'll see a person with a table and an old desktop computer, and you give him your USB or your micro-SD and he'll load it up for you. I'd say this is almost entirely how music is being distributed within Africa. Physical formats are over. It's been about five or six years since people stopped putting out stuff on tape.

So I guess people sort of skipped the CD and went straight from tape to MP3?

Exactly. The same way people skipped land-lines and went straight to mobile phones. We're going to put some stuff out on SD card, actually. The SD card's nice, there's still a physical

thing to it and SD cards are very useful here. You can package it nicely into some kind of interesting format.

Why did you guys decide to concentrate on tape as a format?

It's so quick, it's so easy, it's so fast, and it can sound so good, especially if you do the right mastering on it. And you can fit a lot more music on it than on an equivalent vinyl release. We're never going to stop making tapes. And one shouldn't underestimate the small but meaningful income stream that a DIY tape release can make, compared to just putting it on Spotify.

With vinyl, you have to wait, you're kind of divorced from the whole process, unless you do lathe cutting and stuff like that, which obviously is getting more popular. I think over the next few years, people will realise, oh wow, I can put this out on tape. People are going to realise it is in their interest and advantage to have control. People are so disconnected – "I make music, but what do I do with it now?". At least in Europe there are still some DIY routes. Bandcamp, even. But even Bandcamp can be challenging in Africa. It's hard to get on to PayPal if you have an African address.

In terms of production costs, we do take a hit, in the overarching operations of everything we do, the cost of running the label. I mean, it's a question of where you draw the line. Is it the whole incubation process, the ecosystem? Music gets generated through our residency programme, so in that sense the costs are huge. But the direct costs to the label are small compared to running a festival. And the advantages are so big: you're getting exposure for that artist, they're touring, they're putting music out...

What is the funding situation like in Uganda?

The early 2000s were a sort of bonanza. There was money available for cultural start-ups and organisations, and sadly a lot of it was badly spent, I think. Not to blow our own trumpet, but I think we've shown that you can do a lot of things with very little money. I don't think money was what was missing, in many ways. You need a little bit of money to do interesting cultural stuff, but you don't need a lot.

So what was missing?

I think what was missing was more seed money being used to start culturally sustainable projects. Or financially sustainable cultural projects. Because there have been too many cases of great projects starting in Africa, and then, as soon as the aid gets cut, or the funding gets cut, then it's over. You need just to figure out ways to stay afloat in a challenging environment with few income streams available. But when you had, say, a ten year grant, and 200,000 euros every year, there was a bit less incentive to be financially sustainable.

Where do you locate yourselves in relation to the NGO panorama, to broader questions of development?

Well, I think we're more of a homegrown CBO, a community-based organisation. Everything's quite organic, in terms of the way it works. It started organically and has grown organically, in step with the means we have. We try not to rely on funding. If it's there, great, there's plenty more we could do if we had extra means. But if it isn't, it doesn't make a difference to what we do.

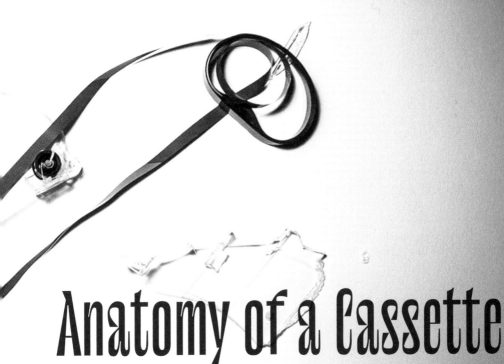

Anatomy of a Cassette

Talking to contemporary cassette practitioners, one thing that comes through again and again is their appreciation of the physicality, the materiality of the tape itself. There are several factors that might lie behind this. A highly satisfactory form, the cassette (or, more precisely, the case) is in fact a phi rectangle, a shape known since ancient times for its harmonious properties. Fitting neatly in your palm or pocket, it exerts the fascination of all things miniature, particularly relative to the LP, next to which it looks like a Chihuahua alongside an Afghan Hound. In this chapter, we will break the cassette down into its various components, consider each one in isolation, and then put them all back together again. In the process we will show that some of tape's appeal stems from the properties of its individual parts, as well as their harmonious interaction.

CASE

Tapes come in cases. These are usually made up of two plastic pieces connected by a ball-and-socket hinge: the lid, usually transparent, which holds the cassette and the inlay and swings open like a little door, and the frame, which can be made of coloured or transparent plastic. There are a range of subtle variations on this theme, but commercial tape releases tend to stick to it closely.

Some tapes, however, come in cardboard cases – cassette singles often only had a cardboard sleeve from which they were pushed in and out. The truth is, the case is mainly for decoration and storage purposes. The irregular shape of the cassette cartridge itself means that you cannot easily pile them on top of each other. Likewise, storing them upright, library-style, as you would with CDs, is impossible unless they are in cases.

The case is in fact a protective covering of a protective covering. While both vinyl and CD need to be protected on pain of death from dirt and scratches, the cassette itself is quite robust and can survive perfectly well without its case. The spooled tape, its delicate entrails, make it vulnerable when in use, and eventually decays, but otherwise the format is extraordinarily resilient. In consequence, designers of experimental tape packaging have great freedom to reinterpret the basic model – say, as a dirty sock, to take one particularly outré example from the back catalogue of musician Eugene Chadbourne.

Two monumental cassette releases, detailed below, will serve to give a sense of the plastic possibilities inherent in the tape case form. On top of that, they show how different projects have been exploring similar approaches and techniques throughout the many decades of cassette culture's existence.

The first release was put out in 1985 by the seminal Newcastle, UK, band :zoviet-france:, a double album called *Popular Soviet Songs and Youth Music*. The case (packaging) was highly elaborate. The tapes fit inside a sculpted ceramic box. A seabird feather was pushed through holes in both box and cassettes and then stuck in place with sealing wax, so you had to break it to get the tapes out. Inserts included a silk-screened US flag with hammers and sickles in place of stars, and a set of elaborate inlay cards.

The second release came 29 years later, when Manchester, UK, label Sacred Tapes put out *Archive Box #001,* a box set of their first six albums, black cassettes encased in a handmade cube of Brutalist concrete. The cube has a lift-off concrete lid silk-screened with the title, and contains a set of inlay cards printed with a risograph.

The overlap in aesthetic approach between these two productions does not need to be spelled out. Suffice to say, the inessential nature of the cassette case leaves a lot of room for creative reimagining.

INLAY

The inlay or j-card is the card or paper tucked inside the lid of the case. There are two broad categories of cassette inlay, one that comes pre-printed and one left largely blank.

The first accompanies formal musical releases. They usually bear the cover and additional information, and are folded in such a way as to create a spine. The cover is usually a reworking of the LP version, if there is one, adapted somehow to the rectangularity of the cassette. The best are those that survive the transformation from LP/canvas to cassette/cameo by becoming something more than a shrunk-down version.

SAC #001

STUSHEVATSYA
LOST SEIZURES FROM A DISINTEGRATED NATION

C20
QTV20

Side A
1. Creak of Broken Veins
2. Centre of a Glass State

Side B
3. Remnants of a Slaughtered People

One of many alter' tales on by Tombed Vision label head David McLean (Punctum, Aging, River Slaughter), Stushevatsya arrives at a focal point for his excursions into more sample based work.

Built with multiple layers of twisted and warped field recordings, the 3 tracks on 'Lost Seizures From a Disintegrated Nation' form a cohesive display amounting to something that can confidently be described as beautiful sitting amongst a genre dominated by noise.

Written and recorded by David McLean

BASF

SM LH cassette

stereo
CASSETTE

BASF

LH SM cassette

2 x 30 min

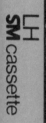

88 m

BASF 60

60
88 m

88 m

low noise

OR OM

OM K 60

AGFA
SUPERCHROM

AGFA SUPERCHROM

HiFi SuperFerro

SWITZERLAND

ICM

HiFi nach
DIN 45500

60

| Cr | 60 |
| 70 µs | 2x30 min +6 |

chromdioxid II

SM Compact Cassette HIFI DIN 45500

60
2x30 min +6

60

These inlays often comprise little concertina booklets with textual or visual extra content, typically the lyrics to the songs, to stare at blankly as you listen to the music. The CD's inlay may seem similar to a record – flat and square – but it works much more like this kind of j-card.

The second category of inlay are those that come with blank tapes. These are typically only one piece of card printed on two sides. The outward-facing sides of blank cassettes are almost always glorious examples of period branding; many image archives exist from different decades and continents, each one a treasure trove of graphic design. The inside tended to have more blank space, often lined.

Blank tape j-cards needed to do two things. One, call the eye of shoppers, which was the job of the lurid branding. Two, provide space for people to write the details of whatever they recorded onto the tape itself. A successful j-card was one that combined these functions harmoniously.

A sub-category of this type of inlay is of course the self-same j-cards after they have been written on or otherwise customised. There are myriad ways to go about this. At one extreme is the ornate, profuse look, doodles and elaborate typographical experimentation, stickers and collages. Here, the goal is to personalise the inlay as fully as possible, creating a Duchampian one-off. From a faceless commodity, the tape is transformed into a handmade object.

At the other extreme are people for whom the tape and j-card are strictly functional items, with only the bare minimum of relevant information scrawled on them. Recall that, for all its musical and creative applications, the blank tape was first and foremost a functional item. For every CAR MIX 1996, there were three tapes recorded inside

SILURE ALBINOS

ppâts pour Carpes et Gros Poissons Vol.1

FISHING CLUB

RAIN RAIN

TOGENKYO / フレデリック

C M O T I O N N E S

MOTIONS

QUETZAL EP

HARVEY
RUSHMORE
AND THE
OCTOPUS

Plïnkï Plønkï
Happy Birthday

Plïnkï Plønkï Happy Birthday

PCR004

PATRICK GIBIN

VOL 06

ALTERED
SOUL
EXPERIMENT

PATRICK GIBIN

.A.'J

ALTERED
SOUL
EXPERIMENT

ASL-06

D.T.

DEMO

++ VALERIO MOSCATELLI · TENTACOLI +

MII

Boris Barksdale

dingy police station interview rooms, the inlay carelessly inscribed with only a number and a name.

Finally, inside blank cassettes there would sometimes be a small sheet of stickers. There would typically be two long white strips to write the name of the album on, and a selection of other smaller stickers, including 'A' and 'B' and sometimes 'MASTER' and 'SLAVE', a problematic terminology used to differentiate between the original cassette and subsequent copies (and suggesting how the companies that produced them expected people to be making many copies of the same tape).

CARTRIDGE

Lastly, there is the cassette itself, the plastic cartridge that contains the spool of magnetic tape. The basic structure of all tapes is absolutely uniform in order to ensure they are compatible with every kind of tape player. All feature two holes corresponding to two spools, the supply and the take up (roles that alternate depending on which side is being played). Then there are smaller elements related to playback, among them the capstan and pinch-roller openings, the tape guides, the pressure pad, and the magnetic shield. And of course there is the write-protect tab on the top edge, which when broken off allows the tape to be recorded over. These delicate and precise components work together in finely tuned harmony; the robust carapace of the cassette belies the complexity and intricacy of its internal mechanism.

There are myriad varieties of cartridge. The plastic it is made from can be clear, tinted, or solid and hence opaque, or indeed a combination of these elements (for example, a mainly opaque body with a transparent plastic strip lengthwise across the middle). The clear or tinted plastic cartridges can of course be seen through, enabling

Cassette cartridges of different colours. *Image courtesy of Sara Valentino.*

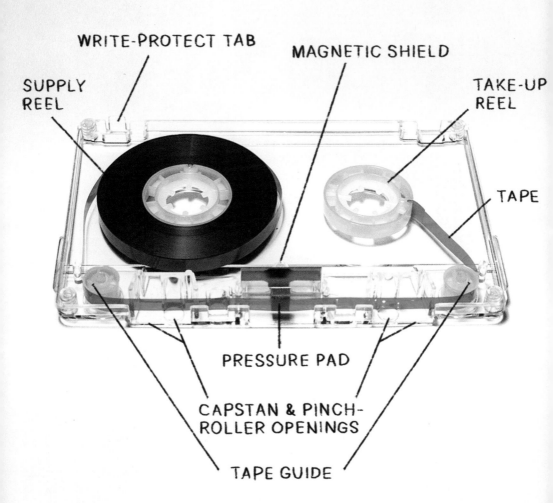

WRITE-PROTECT TAB

MAGNETIC SHIELD

SUPPLY
REEL

TAKE-UP
REEL

TAPE

PRESSURE PAD

CAPSTAN & PINCH-
ROLLER OPENINGS

TAPE GUIDE

Anatomy of a cassette: the components of a compact cassette.

listeners to orientate themselves approximately as to where they are in the recording. Those that are made of solid plastic often come with a little window in the space between the two spools, with the same end. The only limitations to the design possibilities of cassette cartridges are the limitations of the material itself. In short, you can get any visual effect out of the tapes that you can get out of plastic – they can be glossy, matt, iridescent, sparkly or glittery, and of virtually any colour.

Most tapes are emblazoned in some way with details of the recording they hold. This could be via words printed directly onto the body, or some sort of adhesive. In fact, many tapes will be covered almost completely by stickers with the name of the album, record label and so on.

THE SUM OF ITS PARTS

What are we talking about when we talk about tape? As noted, the term 'cassette tape' brings together the two essential components that make up the final product (a little like 'spork' does, for example). For a cassette to be a cassette it needs both a cartridge and a spool of magnetic tape. Unlike 'vinyl record', 'cassette tape' is thus not as redundant as it sounds, and to say either 'cassette' or 'tape' is in a way to foreground either form or function.

Building on this, it's worth taking a moment to think about the relationship of the recording to the format, in particular by triangulating the tape with other music media. In the case of a digital file, track and format are indistinguishable – the song is the MP3, and the MP3 is the song. MP3s are no more than a series of bits, and what you have in iTunes is simply a list of file names. In the case of vinyl, meanwhile, music and format are distinguishable. Indeed, the format itself defines the experience of listening: before you start, you have to perform a series of micro-calisthenics that are unique to putting on a record. Then, the sound when the needle first touches the vinyl is almost as integral to the experience as the music itself, like the tap of baton on podium at the start of a concert.

The tape shares similarities with both. Like the MP3, the tape was meant in its day to be frictionless, interchangeable and disposable. Artist Joep Van Liefland observes of the VHS that it is "the minimalist object par excellence": "abstract, serial, hermetic, industrial".[22] We could readily apply these epithets to the cassette. Obsolescence, however, or the passage of time has given the tape a certain personality, a certain aura. Unlike the MP3, but like the record, it has transcended its own industrial use value; where it was previously an abstract quality, the tape has grown a soul. (Perhaps a format's true, innate qualities only become apparent once it is obsolete – people didn't realise that a record sounded like a record until they heard a CD, and vinyl's real death knell didn't come until Portishead and Tricky began using crackle and hiss to add texture to their tracks. John Cage and Co., meanwhile, were not very conscious of the format-specific sonic qualities of magnetic tape – Cage appears to think of tape as sound made flesh, more than a specific, bounded platform.)

A significant part of the cassette's new-found aura comes from the different parts that accompany it. Those elements that are nominally superfluous (the case, j-card, etc.) in fact are an important source of the colour and charisma of each release. Online streaming services, by contrast, strip all that information away, leaving only the name of the song and the artist. Some services provide the album title and, if you're lucky, a thumbnail of the cover art, but it seems that a key pillar of the digital strategy is to dissolve albums away like bread in a duck pond, reordering an artist's work into an algorithmic ranking of their 'top tracks'.

What does this achieve? One effect is to reduce music to discrete, interchangeable units, definitively digital products, denuded of all history and context. Without the production details (producer, band members, year and place of recording) there is a feeling that these songs just appeared out of nowhere, AI-generated using models derived from big data. Theodor Adorno makes a similar observation regarding books printed without any paratextual information, such as date and place of publication. Without this, he says, books are robbed of their *principium individuationis*, becoming "mere exemplars of a species... drug[s] on a market".[23]

Part of the enduring appeal of the cassette, like that of the LP, is that paramusical details are not supressed as commercially irrelevant. The cassette is a way to reclaim music, make it more than indistinguishable data to be listlessly scrolled through. The case and j-card make music palpably human, explicitly anchored to a concrete time and space, the fruit of a collaboration between musician, producer and recording studio.

A cassette, then, is a whole rich package, case plus inlay plus cartridge plus recording. It is more than the sum of its parts, and that excess value is precisely the numinous quality that has guaranteed its relevance following the expiry of its *sensu stricto* use value – a relevance that the MP3 will not have in a few years' time, both for functional reasons, and simply because there's so little that's human about it.

Following pages:
Mix Tapes, Photoshop,
Wacom Tablet, 2012.
*Illustration by Bungo
Design, behance.com/
bungodesign.*

GLUE OF THE WORLD

mixtape
/ˈmɪksteɪp/ 🔊

noun

a compilation of favourite pieces of music, typically by many different artists, recorded on to tape or another medium by an individual.

01 Sometimes I go to yard sales to buy cassettes compiled by people who are complete strangers to me. You see something that has 'Marty's Mix' scrawled on it in ballpoint pen. You take it home and you don't know if it's going to be US post-punk hardcore or Kenny Rogers. Whatever it is, though, I know I'm getting a slice of someone's life. Cassettes are the only format that can give you that. 02 The mix tape is a form of American folk art: predigested cultural artifacts combined with homespun technology and magic markers turns the mix tape into a message in a bottle. I am no mere consumer of pop culture, it says, but also a producer of it. Mix tapes mark the moment of consumer culture in which listeners attained control over what they hear, in what order and at what cost... The mix tape is a list of quotations, a poetic form in fact: the cento is a poem made up of lines pulled from other poems. The new poet collects and remixes. **03 Over the last 25 years the mix tape has become a paradigmatic form of popular expression. It is one part Victorian flower album, one part commonplace book, one part collage, and one part recital. The maker dubs onto cassette or burns onto CD a group of songs by other hands, the selection and sequence intended to compose a billet-doux, score a dance party, prove a point, or simply demonstrate the compiler's taste and expertise... The mix tape can be transitive – a letter – or intransitive – a diary entry. It can follow a particular**

line or expansively juxtapose. It can be ruled by sound or by concept. It is almost always fleeting – often more so than the songs it comprises – and endures best as a time capsule of a vibe gone by. 04 To me, making a tape is like writing a letter – there's a lot of erasing and rethinking and starting again. A good compilation tape, like breaking up, is hard to do. You've got to kick off with a corker, to hold the attention ... and then you've got to up it a notch, or cool it a notch, and you can't have white music and black music together, unless the white music sounds like black music, and you can't have two tracks by the same artist side by side, unless you've done the whole thing in pairs and ... oh, there are loads of rules. 05 **Say you made a 120-minute cassette: forget about collecting the songs and all the artwork and labeling. You basically sat in front of a machine and recorded it. You'd wait for each song to end and then you'd hit stop. When you received a tape like that, you felt the weight of somebody's investment in those songs and in the time they put to make something for you... If you were a girl and I wanted... to show you I like you, I would make you a 90-minute cassette wherein I would show off my tastes. I would play you a musical theater song next to a hip-hop song next to an oldie next to some pop song you maybe never heard, also subliminally telling you how much I like you with all these songs. I think I learned more about writing scores for**

Broadway by making mixtapes in the '90s than I did in college. You're learning about rise and fall and energy and tempo shifts. You're showing off your taste and your references. You're trying to be witty... through placement of music you didn't write... 06 We made a lot of mix tapes while we were together. Tapes for making out, tapes for dancing, tapes for falling asleep. Tapes for doing the dishes, for walking the dog. I kept them all. I have them piled up on my bookshelves, spilling out of my kitchen cabinets, scattered all over the bedroom floor. I don't even have pots or pans in my kitchen, just that old boombox on the counter, next to the sink. So many tapes. **07 The mixtape is both personal and an expression of technological will to power – an intervention that occurs not outside but against and within power relations that structure music listening. But mostly, the mixtape is heralded as a personal expression, even if that communication is based on appropriation... The mixtape compiles bits of recordings from the producer's collection, and tries to target its audience of one, either through didacticism, showing off, trying to match up interests, etc. It conveys something of the character of the person making it, in theory, as well as being a display of commodity ownership, as opposed to copyright ownership, through creative juxtaposition. This investment (including when the tape is destined for your own use) means the mix takes on the character of**

a snapshot, and like Barthes' idea of the photographic image, it suggests narratives beyond it. 08 The mixtape allowed a consumer to get quality and variety all in one, and the best new music first. This is also a major factor in what made downloading music from the Internet attractive. The consumer could become the producer – selecting the song titles they wanted, compiling them on one 'album', if they liked; when they liked; and as soon as the music was released, anywhere in the world. Say Amen. **09 This music is the glue of the world, Mark. It's what holds it all together. Without this, life would be meaningless.**

TRACKLIST
01 Thurston Moore, in Pete Paphides – 'Thinking inside the (plastic) box: Still cherished by mix-tape romantics, the cassette isn't ready to die, says Pete Paphides', *The Times*, 18 December 2009, p. 8
02 Matias Viegener – 'The mix tape is a form of American folk art', in: Moore (ed.) – *Mix Tape: The Art of Cassette Culture*, 2005, p. 35
03 Luc Sante – 'Disco Dreams', in: *New York Review of Books*, 13 May 2004
04 Nick Hornby – *High Fidelity*, 1995, p. 88 f.
05 *Hamilton* musical creator Lin-Manuel Miranda speaking on NPR, 3 January 2017
06 Rob Sheffield – *Love Is a Mix Tape: Life, Loss, and What I Listened to*, 2007, p. 3
07 Paul Hegarty – 'The Hallucinatory Life of Tape', in: *Culture Machine*, vol. 9, 2007
08 Cedric Muhammad – 'The MixTape: The End of an Era?', www.CedricMuhammad.com, 12 September 2010
09 *Empire Records*, 1995

NUMBER 9

IT

2-477-564-01®

EXPERIMENTAL

TAPE MUSIC

ALL THE THING WAS MADE WITH
LOOPS. I HAD ABOUT 30 LOOPS
GOING, FED THEM ONTO ONE
BASIC TRACK. I WAS GETTING
CLASSICAL TAPES, GOING UPSTAIRS
AND CHOPPING THEM UP, MAKING
IT BACKWARDS AND THINGS LIKE
THAT, TO GET THE SOUND EFFECTS.
ONE THING WAS AN ENGINEER'S
TESTING VOICE SAYING, 'THIS IS
EMI TEST SERIES NUMBER NINE.'
I JUST CUT UP WHATEVER HE SAID
AND I'D NUMBER NINE IT.

John Lennon, on how he made 'Revolution No. 9'

The Beatles' 'Revolution No. 9' is a landmark in experimental tape
music. As sinister as it is silly, this 'song' constitutes an eight-
and-a-half minute collage of at least 45 different sound sources,
most of them tape-based. It is also almost certainly the most well-
known piece of Musique Concrète ever made, a fact that may well
have proven vexing to the godfathers of the genre.

Musique Concrète is a style or philosophy of music focused on what today might be called field recordings or 'found sounds'. One of its pioneers was Pierre Schaeffer, a French engineer turned musician who co-founded the Groupe de Recherche de Musique Concrète in 1951. Schaeffer's approach was based on collecting 'concrete' sounds that he found in everyday life, then using techniques like tape looping and splicing to abstract them into compositions. He was at the forefront of a movement in which, as John Cage put it, "magnetic tape was used not simply to record performances of music, but to make a new music that was possible only because of it".[24]

It is interesting to note that the early (pre-cassette) tape recorders were not marketed primarily for music reproduction. Instead, advertising focused on their ability to capture sounds and create an acoustic analogue to home photography, which was then becoming accessible on the home market. Record everything from baby crying to grandpa snoring, guide books advised. One noted how sound "remains vivacious and binds people together more forcefully than any picture. In a person's voice we encounter his personal moods; in the sound of a running machine we can hear force and speed; the sound of birds connects us with nature".[25] In short, the producers of the first domestic tape devices thought that the world was ready for a revolution in domestic Musique Concrète. They were wrong, as it happens, and tape didn't really capture the attention of the masses until the advent of the cassette.

TAPE MUSIC MEDIUM

Early followers of Schaeffer included Edgard Varèse and Karlheinz Stockhausen, whose Kontakte (1958) is scored for "piano, percussion and 4-track tape". By the mid-1960s, tape was the foremost tool of the musical avant-garde, above all in the US, where in 1962 Morton Subotnick and Ramon Sender founded the San Francisco Tape Music Center, "a place to learn about work within the tape music medium". Steve Reich was involved in the project. His first tape composition,

'It's Gonna Rain' (1964), is still bewitching. To create it, Reich took two identical loops from the same field recording of a street preacher and played them alongside each other. Minute discrepancies between the two machines meant that the two versions slipped out of sync. So Reich explored the so-called phasing effect, lining up different combinatory variations of the two loops.

Reich was a foundational influence on Brian Eno, inspiring him to create, in collaboration with Robert Fripp, a system known as Frippertronics. This features two reel-to-reel tape recorders set up alongside each other, with the supply reel of the first machine connected to the take-up reel of the second in a sort of lemniscate. Music is recorded onto one, and, after a delay, passed on to the second, then ping-ponged back to the first with extra audio elements overlaid on top, creating a dense impasto of sound. In the liner notes of the album *Discreet Music* (1975), Eno calls this technique "the long delay echo system with which I have experimented since I became aware of the musical possibilities of tape recorders in 1964". This was the year when 'It's Gonna Rain' was released, but it was also the year after Delia Derbyshire's *Doctor Who* theme music was first heard, a compelling and evocative exercise in tape looping and distortion.

During this period tape was also used as a tool for experimentation in the literary field, perhaps most notably by William Burroughs and Samuel Beckett.[26] Burroughs in particular used tape extensively (in fact, doesn't his famed 'cut-up' technique constitute a tardy application of basic Musique Concrète principles to a literary context?). He was also convinced that tape could be used as a tool for actual social revolution, both "AS A FRONT LINE WEAPON TO PRODUCE AND ESCALATE RIOTS" and "AS A LONG RANGE WEAPON TO SCRAMBLE AND NULLIFY ASSOCIATIONAL LINES PUT DOWN BY MASS MEDIA".[27] The first may be wishful thinking, but the second of these possibilities could be taken as a credo for the cassette cultures that were to evolve out of these early explorations of the potentialities of tape.

A mash-up is similar to but not the same as a collage. A mash-up is a fusion in which disparate elements dissolve into a harmonious or at least coherent whole, as in Danger Mouse's *Grey Album* (2004), to take a representative example. Collage, when it isn't pure decoration, does the opposite – jar, surprise, provoke.

Collage is the fundamental operation of tape-based sound experimentation. While the ability to overlay one sound over another requires a degree of investment in the craft, with a single-deck hi-fi even children could and did splice together different clips, producing sound collages that Burroughs would have been proud of.

In fact, it may be easier to produce true collage with a mechanical as opposed to a digital interface. Computers are so effortlessly complex that when it comes to juxtaposing sound or image it is hard to reproduce the impact of cuts made laboriously by hand. John Lennon getting up and walking upstairs to play just one loop might seem absurdly primitive compared to the programming software we take for granted today. But, as with all things analogue, working with tape forces you to take your time. The enduring resonance of 'Revolution No. 9' comes in part from the fact that each element was carefully, deliberately weighed and chosen – literally handpicked.

Nevertheless, by the 1980s digital tools for generating and processing sound were supplanting analogue technology, and in the 1990s it became clear that magnetic tape in general and cassettes in particular would never again occupy such a prominent place at the forefront of sonic experimentation.

CASSETTE AS PERFORMANCE

One field, however, in which the cassette is still used as an instrument in its own right is that of performance, and performatively composed music. Here, there is a rich tradition that can be traced back to German cult band Tangerine Dream, who seem to have been the first to integrate tape loops into their live act. Founding member Conrad Schnitzler, a hugely influential figure, went on to create the Kassettenorgel or Cassette organ, which consisted of six stereo tape decks with which he would build up carefully layered walls of sound.

The PORTABLE BOOED USIC BUSKING UNIT NUCLEAR BRAIN PHYSICS SURGERY SCHOOL LAB PHILOSOPHER'S UNION MEMBER'S MOUTHPIECE BLATNERPHONE HALLUCINOMAT worked on a similar principle. It was invented in 1988 by Baltimore's tENTATIVELY, a cONVENIENCE for use in his famously anarchic performances. It was "a concrete mixing studio featuring a suitcase filled with forty pounds worth of electronics, four cassette players, a backpack with four 40 watt speakers, a video camera, VCR player, two drumsticks, a cymbal perched atop a ball point pen, and a box that held up to 60 tapes (including recordings of a conspiracy theory radio show, dogs yowling, blades of grass being blown over, and snippets of a BBC 'transitions and cues' tape)".[28]

That wild, haphazard, promiscuous approach still holds sway among practitioners of tape music. Japanese composer and performer Aki Onda has spent the last 20 years using Walkmans to compile an archive of field recordings. In site-specific performances, the artist uses these tapes to build up what he calls a "sonic collage of ritualistic tape music", abstract soundscapes that are at once disorientating and oddly warming, like all the best tape-based music. Liz Harris, who records as Grouper, also mines tapes for uncanny effects, as for example in her *Violet Replacement* (2008), which blends vocals, tape loops, field recordings and snippets of Wurlitzer. Playing live, she alternates live instruments with pedals and tape-based sounds, sitting alongside a table covered in cassettes that she picks up and works with seemingly almost at random. Then there is non-horse, a "tape manipulation anti-brainwashing music project", which, according to the Bandcamp of creator G. Lucas Crane, "symbolizes the hollowing out of meaning that occurs with the use and manipulation of language and my desire to combat this by mixing forgotten sonics on broken unpopular deployment systems. A tape recorder", he continues, "is an externalized section of the human nervous system".

Other contemporary artists use cassettes and cassette players in an even more self-enclosed way. Stephen Cornford's installation *Binatone Galaxy* features 30 old portable cassette players, attached to the walls. Instead of cassettes, these machines contain contact microphones that pick up the sound of their own microscopic functioning. Together, they create a beguiling soundscape that suggests everything from flowing water to construction work.

Cassette Life, pencil, guache and collage. *Illustration by Derek Brazell*.

"Although externally illogical, our anti-releases serve as a form of audio/visual provocation that attempts to force interaction on the part of the listener by implementing tangible manifestations of abstract concepts. While seemingly unplayable in their presented state, the intention is that the consumer will actively seek a solution to playback rather than settle for the notion they are 'art objects'. Our anti-releases often focus on the topic of creation/destruction, but each is governed by a strict enforcement of principles which we stand by. The first being that there must always be actual, consciously created audio/visual material contained within, and the second being that the material must be playable or salvageable in some form." **Auris Apothecary**

Since 1999, Alexis Malbert (aka Tapetronic) has been recycling and transforming audio cassettes and tape recorders to make machines that play music. Inventor, among other things, of the Scratchette, the Vibro-K7, the Audio-Skate and the Wheeling Walkmen, he acts directly on mechanical devices, using gestures as a source of energy, to produce strange and dynamic music.

William Basinski is probably the most celebrated practitioner of tape-based music working today. His *Disintegration Loops* series stems from the moment in 2011 when he came to record some of his old tape loops from the 1970s. When he put the first one on, Basinski realised that the tape was decaying in real time, right before his ears. So he hit record, and the resulting suite redefined tape music.

YOU HOLD IT IN YOUR HANDS

William Basinski, illustration by Vincenzo Suscetta.

Of course, when I started, that's what you used. I was recording my masters on cassette. *Shortwave Music* and *The River* and all those were recorded live with analogue reel-to-reel decks and mixing loops, then mastered to cassette in my little home studio, first in San Francisco and then New York, where we moved in 1980. I didn't really know what I was doing back then except that I was getting results and I really liked it. And as someone who was trained in classical music, I knew composition. I was just trying to be a composer. I didn't know if I really was one or not. But I liked what I was doing. All my friends were painters, so they're painting in their studios and I'm in my studio, painting with sound and grabbing things out of the airwaves, and slowing them down, and finding whole universes of melancholy deep within this sappy Muzak. Once you dial it down and look under the microscope it's like, oh, yeah. That's what's under there.

San Francisco has one of the richest soundscapes of any city I've ever been in. There's something unique, so beautiful. It's these seven hills surrounded by water and there's fog frequently.

So you've got all this water and water vapour kind of holding in the sounds of the city. You've got creaking cable cars and you've got electronic buses with what we'd call cricket legs, and they put out kind of static-y stuff, you've got fog horns and you've got just your usual traffic sounds and other things. But it's a very, very rich soundscape, you could just record it and make a record of it. Very inspiring for me.

I always say the most important class I had in music school was the contemporary music class, where our teacher taught us about, for example, John Cage, and I learned you don't have to write everything down and orchestrate it. You can use tape, you can use radios, you can... do nothing. Steve Reich's early tape loop and delay things came out, and *Drumming*, and the other ones. And then when he translated that loop and feedback loop thing into *Music for Eighteen Musicians*, his first major masterpiece, we were all like, wow. So there was the second point. And then when Eno's *Music for Airports* came out, so melancholy, so beautiful, that was the third point of the golden triangle that gave me licence to do what I needed to do as a melancholy child.

Then, looking at the back of *Discreet Music*, there's a diagram of Frippertronics, the tape delay system with two decks, and so I was like, oh. Went to the junk store round the corner in San Francisco, found two big old 1960s Norelco Philips flatbed, portable, 40-pound tape decks. Five dollars each. And a box of old tapes. Ten dollars. OK. So I went home and started cutting things up and making loops and preparing the piano I was renting at the time. Putting microphones in this old '50s refrigerator we had, in the freezer, oh my god, the compressors, oh, on those old things, you record them at high speed and turn it down and you've got massive, like, universal, like, outer space drones and

frequencies you'd never heard before. And all kinds of stuff. It just creates itself. So they were all painting and I was painting. You're working with your hands, working with basically organic materials. You know, tape is oil-based plastic, probably rabbit-based glue, and rust. The first thing that goes away is the glue and that's what happened when I was archiving my loops in 2001, and that ended up becoming *The Disintegration Loops*. The rabbit died.

The Disintegration Loops was a two-day session that just blew my mind, and over the course of that session, I went from countermelodies and creating new compositions with these loops to stay out of the way, let it do what it needs to do, it doesn't need counter-melodies, it's doing what it wants, just make sure you're recording it. So, you know, you watch someone die. You love them, you're there with them, you have to just... be there. And it's intense. And then you remember them. You bury them and there's that hole in your heart.

The thing that was such an epiphany for me, I was at a point in my life before *The Disintegration Loops* where I was broke, I closed my shop, I didn't have any money, I was about to lose my loft, and it was a beautiful summer day in August, and I didn't know what to do, no work coming in. I read this little turquoise *Way of Zen* book by Alan Watts. So I'm sitting on my couch in this beautiful sun, in this beautiful old Arcadia loft, and I'm like, you dumbass, get off your ass, go in the studio, get back to work. I had this new thing called a CD burner. Get in there, these tapes are all going to die, you better archive them before they do. Well, that's what got me in there. But then when they did what they did, and they disintegrated one by one in their own time, in their own way, and I managed to record it, I suddenly had this Catholic epiphany. I just recorded the life and death of these melodies and they're redeemed to a new medium. So it was a profound moment for me.

But I'm not constantly trying to redo this kind of thing. It's a constant worry with these old loops that I had, that I created, they're my patches, they're not digital, they're analogue. I still have many but a lot of them were made with used tape that I bought in the late '70s, so they're fragile, and you've got to get them on the first pass if you want to get what's in there.

I have my tools, and I have my techniques, but it's different for every piece. Part of my technique is hoping that some random spark will come in and create a mistake. Mistakes can be great. They can also be horrible and we hate that. But sometimes it's like, OK, we've got to go with it, we got a scar, OK, we'll make it work.

In terms of devices, those Norelco machines, for me and for what I did and do, are particularly good, because they are earlier consumer models, they have four speeds, they were basically like the iPods of the day. They were for old white guys to make their playlists on and they could do it on the slow speed so that when the babe came over they didn't have to get up to change the record, for hours on one reel. And they don't have any extra doodads on there that, like, if the tape stops there's this thing that makes it turn off. On those kinds of machines you have to disable that little motherfucker or your tape loop won't go around.

So these old things are great, they're just plain, there's nothing moderating the tape so you get a lot of wow and flutter and stuff like that. It's not a professional recording device. But that's what I liked and that's what I needed and that's what I used; that's what I could afford. If you keep your loops tight, they won't chew them up in the machine. I used D batteries: they're heavy and round and keep the tape loop tight, they're not too magnetised so they won't get yanked into the machine.

Using tape today is a choice. But tape is analogue. You're recording the actual thing. It's like film, it's not sampled… That's what you're hearing. So it has a beauty and a warmth to it. So people can hear and I think feel it. Your eye – your brain – recognises film differently than it does video. You actually look around a film. It's light and shadow. With video you're just sort of hypnotised.

Young people are buying cassettes now, which is very interesting. I don't even know, do people even make cassette players any more? How do they play them? I have tons of old cassette players, they're all broken. My young assistant Preston loves it, he has a 4-track. Young people like it. And I guess I've had an influence in certain ways from the work that I've managed to do over the years, so we'll see. Everything old is new again. Tape, you hold it in your hands, you cut it when you're making loops, you use a pair of scissors. You tape it, and you hold it, and you put it on the thing. It can break. It can get crunched up, or chewed up by a cat, or, you know, disintegrate.

Current custodian of the legendary Staaltape label, Rinus van Alebeek uses Walkmans to execute spellbinding sound performances in repurposed warehouses and community spaces.

THE PRACTICE OF SOUND

There was a time in the '90s when I was in an airplane quite often, travelling here and there. So I bought a very expensive Walkman – the black metal Sony, the little brother of the Sony Pro. And it came with a microphone. That's when it first occurred to me to make recordings.

I went to live in Italy, to work as an assistant to a conceptual artist, helping him make things. Attached to the house we were living in was a little church with nice acoustics. One day we went in there to make recordings, using the sounds we could find in the church itself, with the objects that were there. I think that was one of my first experimental recordings. There were four of us, just making sounds, moving furniture, doing stuff. And listening back to it. I don't know where it came from, but suddenly I started doing this. This was in the mid-'90s.

Then for six years I was only recording. The microphone on the little Sony Walkman is very small, so it can go anywhere – stick it in a tube, any object you can think of, put it on a surface and turn the recording level very high, then create little events like

Rinus van Alebeek, illustration by Vincenzo Suscetta.

this, scratching the table, and it's enormously loud and distorted. Put it on a metal surface and start to rub the metal. Make little sounds close to it or far away.

I record when I feel like recording. For example, I recently moved to a new place. There's a balcony, it's on the third floor, the traffic is very far away, so there's a constant hum, broken up by sounds like crows or church bells. My idea was to start a series of recordings from the same spot, and layer them. So that eventually, in the process the first recording will disappear, and the hum that you have will pile up, so that instead of 10 per cent hum you have 40 per cent hum. But it's very dense hum. It's not a hiss, but it's the hum of the city, amplified. And within it, it's like the dark space at the bottom of the ocean, you've got all these sounds floating around, and higher up the sounds are clearer and freer to move.

So that's one thing I do. Another is just to explore the neighbourhood, find spaces where I put the microphone and listen for three minutes, and that's it. The only plan is to go out walking. I choose a certain walking pace, because with every walking pace your listening experience changes. So first I try to find the right pace, then I start listening while walking, and I think, hm, this could be interesting, not too many cars are passing by, I turn on my microphone for five or six minutes, that's it.

When you listen to it later through the cassette for the first time it becomes immediately hypnotising. You get sucked into it. It's just so relaxing. It sucks you completely into it. I don't know why. Maybe it's because it's a world as it is. I don't have any explanation for it. I've said it before: I think it's the closest we get to time travelling. Because one of the things I've noticed when I make a recording is that when I listen again I can visualise the setting. Everything

becomes visible again. And that was the greatest discovery of making recordings.

You just start to listen. You are on the inside of a globe and there are strict boundaries to it. You hear a strict border of the acoustic space. And, because it is defined as an acoustic space, things within this space start to answer each other. And it's very fascinating to hear this happen, once you sit somewhere and start listening.

In terms of my own performances, I've got several tape machines, from a simple Walkman to a 4-track, sometimes a little Dictaphone with a mini cassette, sometimes an effects pedal connected to one of the machines. Two microphones, one dry and one with reverb. And then I make layers. It can be very lazy and straightforward – quieter and more ambient, like when I make a mix with three or four separate machines. It can be noisy, like when I go over the effect machine and use my Dictaphone, pressing forwards and backwards. Or I have the little Walkman and do all kinds of manipulations, with the tension you can get by pushing the play button half down at the same time as the forward or reverse button, for example, or playing with the pitch, changing the speed – these are all things you can do in very quick succession. You can do it acoustically, and then it becomes a kind of tape dance, because I respond to the sounds with my body, with the movements that I make.

And now I'm moving towards having the sound playing in the background of two or three machines, and concentrating mainly on the things I can do in front of the microphone. I use the pedal for the slow, silent things, I put an endless delay on a tape recording of footsteps, at the slowest speed possible. Then you don't hear the delay any more, just random drum patter, as if it's generating a drum pattern by itself.

If that's very far away, I can overlay my sounds on top of it. It's just a way of listening.

I work with the 4-track – I feed in one or two seconds, or a minute. You can have 20 little pieces, and you work for two or three hours for one minute of sound. It depends on how it comes. You can feed the four tracks with this mosaic of 80 snippets. There's no good sound and no bad sound. There's just sounds that you can use.

It is a very strange process, because I always start with something, I know where to start and I have a general idea of how to continue, but you don't know what's going to happen on the way. So I start with something and then I go through my cassettes and say to one, you have the next sound. And I listen to it and I find the next sound. I don't know how this associative moment comes about. But it happens. It's plain intuition. And another thing – knowing when to stop. Working on a tape composition, if it's going well, stop, and come back to it the next day. You need that unexpected moment when you continue, you need the change of mood, because otherwise you're just hypnotising yourself. You will see, the changes are always radical.

I did a tape run in Berlin, and asked friends to curate them in Paris, Brussels, Montreal. I take a 40-minute tape. I ask ten persons if they want to take part. I set the conditions: you've got four minutes, the work has to be ready in three or four days. You get the tape and you give it by hand to the next person and so on, until it comes back to me again. It prompts people to meet, and it gives a very contemporary snapshot of what is going on in that place at that moment. Because you have to do it from scratch. I release them in editions as small as 12, up to 70 copies, maybe with a few reissues.

There's a lot of young people who use the medium who don't care about nostalgia. It's just there and you can use it. It means freedom, freedom to do what you like. You buy the tape, you record your things on it, you make 30 copies, and you sell the tape. You have the idea yesterday, you have the tape tomorrow. You have 100 per cent control over everything. It's a magic format. Tape is the only medium that I can use. I've tried making music digitally. But in the end it's like dentist's work. Too precise.

The speed of the cassette looks like leisurely walking. I recently discovered one of Tarkovsky's secrets. There's a scene in *The Mirror*, a shot of a river, and the speed of the river is moving at the same speed as his camera. It's also the speed of a cassette turning. This slowly evolving event. It is completely mesmerising.

Tape
Futures

We have already sketched a few possible reasons for tape's appeal among digital natives. However, to really get a handle on that appeal – and appreciate how, far from being a hipster-driven flash in the media pan, the tape revival will continue to go from strength to strength – it may be useful to go deeper into the nitty gritty of the differences between analogue and digital. A good place to start could be Alessandro Ludovico's book *Post-Digital Print* (2012), in which he makes a useful and transferable point: "Digital is the paradigm for content and quantity of information: analogue is the paradigm for usability and interfacing." In other words, digital is like cheap, filling food on the go (the food court in a mall) while analogue is more about flavour and experience (sitting down in a nice restaurant for a meal for two, plus wine).

One might feel that Ludovico is less precise, however, when he goes on to differentiate between formats. "In the case of video", he says, "the medium (whether VHS or DVD) is merely a carrier, since the content is always ultimately displayed on screens. The same is true for music, where cassettes, vinyl records and CDs are only intermediate carriers; the actual listening always happened through speakers".[29]

An MP3 may indeed constitute a mere carrier. But listening via a physical format (or radio) is not only about the music – it is an entire existential experience, one which takes in numerous elements. Ludovico's oversight is to take the way we see things now and project it backwards in time. In reality, it wasn't until the appearance of Napster at the turn of the millennium that people really started to think of music as something that could be detached from the physical realm, its 'carrier', and transformed into a free-floating unit. Prior to this revolutionary turn, the song, the format and the experience of listening were intimately bound up, no more divisible than were the notes from a violin for previous generations. It was not just the track you listened to, but the track plus record plus hi-fi (plus, while we're at it, environmental noise).

For a more nuanced theory of analogue vs digital in the context of musical formats, it makes sense to turn to a musician, specifically Damon Krukowski, whose book *The New Analog* (2017) constitutes a groundbreaking study of what makes the one the one and the other the other. Krukowski hinges his theory on the difference between 'signal' and 'noise'. These of course are technical terms used in music engineering to distinguish between what you actually want to record and listen to (signal) and everything else (noise). An extreme example of noise in action occurs in the final, apocalyptic chord of the Beatles' 'A Day in The Life'. The microphones were turned up so high to record it that they accidentally picked up the noise of the air conditioning system in the studio, which went on to form part of the track.

Previous page:
The Soundwave Transformer's best-known transformation is that of a microcassette recorder. Throughout most of his incarnations, he is an undying loyal lieutenant of the Decepticon leader Megatron. The image is a graphic adaptation of Generation 1 Soundwave box art.

In a more general sense, noise is used to refer to the sound generated simply by the working of recording or playback equipment. Tape noise is a classic example. It was generated at both ends of the process, first when the music was being recorded onto tape-based devices in the studio, and second at home when the music was listened to on cassette.

One key difference between digital and analogue processes and formats resides in their respective treatment of noise. With analogue, even the silence between songs *exists*, is in a technical sense audible as noise. The machine still reads the format even when there is nothing directly recorded onto it, making true silence impossible (similarly to how, in a different way, your heart beating and the thrum of your nervous system make it impossible to ever perceive total silence). Digital, by contrast, simply eliminates noise. Between the songs on a digital recording there is only what engineers refer to as 'digital black', sheer nothingness, neither noise nor signal. Likewise, the recording is only that, a recording, notes scattered against a backdrop of void. As Krukowski puts it, "There is no denying... the increased speed, convenience and low price of digital music delivery. But... it is also an increasingly diminished experience... My digital listening is to signal alone. I hear the notes but not the space between, or the depth below. It's listening to the surface but not the noise".[30]

But isn't noise a fundamentally undesirable element? Well, yes and no. One could think of noise as being like the void set in abstract mathematical theory: it has no value in itself, but without it no other set does either. To return to books, maybe the comparison here is with the paper itself. We could say that the meaning of a book is the printed letters. But without the paper on which they are printed, the letters would in a radical sense not function as communication. As in the musical sphere, precisely what happened with books was that this "noise" was eliminated, the physical specificity of the medium was judged superfluous. And, as in the musical sphere, after

a brief bedazzlement some people seem to be discovering that it is precisely the noise, precisely the part that didn't seem important until it was gone, that maybe even felt like it was holding the signal back from being most fully itself, which is what makes the experience meaningful. Derrida: "Paper... gets hold of us bodily, and through every sense."[31] Krukowski: "Surface noise and tape hiss are not flaws in analog media but artifacts of their use."[32]

To return to our food metaphor, did you ever feel that, no matter which of the panoply of options you choose in the food court, it all somehow ends up sitting in your stomach in the same way, leaving you somewhat satiated, but also a little dissatisfied, antsy, nauseous? This is of course because fast food is a question of variations on the same theme of sweeteners and additives. In an analogous way, for all their many manifestations – films, songs, PDFs, spreadsheets – digital media all constitute variations on the same theme: strings of bits. The main job of the programmes that we use to interface with them is to differentiate one string of bits from another. There is either signal or lack of signal. 1 or 0. Nothing in between.

One clue to the value of noise is to be found in an unexpected place. In a 1997 interview with *Wired* magazine, feminist sociologist Donna Haraway describes how, "If you start talking to people about how they cook their dinner or what kind of language they use to describe trouble in a marriage, you're very likely to get notions of tape loops, communication breakdown, noise and signal".[33] Put differently, human communication involves, even depends on a combination of noise and signal. In fact, it is possible to talk about language itself in those terms. Take the simple phrase 'she eats'. In this phrase, there are two markers to denote that the verb is in the third person singular, namely, the pronoun 'she' and the '-s' tagged on to the base form of the verb – a purely signal-based system would read one of these as redundant noise. This is even more evident in a highly inflected

2XL was the first 'smart-toy' in that it exhibited rudimentary intelligence, memory, game play, and responsiveness.
It is an educational toy robot that was marketed from 1978 to 1981 by the Mego Toy Corporation and then re-introduced by Tiger Electronics in 1992. The '90s version was operated by cassette tapes. The cassette version took advantage of the fact that a cassette has a total of four tracks – one for the left and right channel on each side. The tape head in the player could play any of the four parallel tracks, based on which button was pressed. Playing a 2-XL tape in a standard tape player would result in different audio on the left and right channels, and if the reverse side was played, one would hear the other two tracks being played in reverse. Using all four tracks simultaneously was unique to 2-XL and provided the basis for the interactive give and take.

language like Spanish. The phrase 'los tigres tristes', for example, contains three markers of plurality. If all we cared about was signal, then one marker would be sufficient. But language thrives on noise, on redundancy: it is what distinguishes it from Newspeak.

It would seem to follow that the dialectic of noise and signal corresponds to an innately human mode of communication – of existence, even. According to Krukowski, noise with "its communicative power for the maker, its transformative power for the receiver (...) binds us together in shared time".[34] Far from being redundant or disposable, noise is what makes signal meaningful. Maybe this is why the unending profusion of digital music ultimately fails to satisfy ("Water, water everywhere, / Nor any drop to drink."). And maybe this is why the cassette, like the book or the record, will survive and thrive as a repository and vehicle of true meaning, of human experience.

By way of conclusion it may be appropriate to appropriate, somewhat after the fashion of a mixtape, a visionary argument sketched by Paul Hegarty. In his excellent essay 'The Hallucinatory Life of Tape', Hegarty describes how the Voyager 1 spacecraft, launched in 1977, carried tape recording systems to register things like plasma waves. Thus, "Like the alien in the eponymous film, tape lives on in space". Indeed, the tape continued working perfectly for decades after the launch, which Hegarty attributes to its "being outside of earth's atmosphere, but perhaps also because of its specific mode of functioning, which is to be permanently recording, transmitting and erasing, whilst in continual movement. The Voyager tapes are a far more human artefact", he continues, "than the more famous gold disc with its images, sound recordings etc., which is also on board, for aliens to find. The tape's operation will reveal much more of how humans predominantly construct their existence".[35]

NOTES

1 Bruce Sterling – 'The Dead Media Project: A Modest Proposal and a Public Appeal', in: Tom Whitwell (ed.) – *The Dead Media Notebook: 20th Anniversary Edition*, p. 22

2 Calum Marsh – 'Reconsidering the Revival of Cassette Tape Culture', www.PopMatters.com, 3 December 2009

3 Rosalind Kraus – *A Voyage on the North Sea: Art in the Age of the Post-Medium Condition*, 1999, p. 41

4 John Cage – 'Experimental Music: Doctrine', in: *Silence*, 2015, p. 6

5 Quoted in Damon Krukowski – *The New Analog*, 2017, p. 109

6 See Lyle Owerko – *The Boombox Project: The Machines, the Music, and the Urban Underground*, 2010

7 'The Walkman Effect', in: *Popular Music, Vol. 4, Performers and Audiences*, 1984, pp. 165–180

8 Alfred Schutz – 'Seul contre tous...! Entretien avec Philippe Sollers', in: *Magazine littéraire 171*, April 1976, pp. 50–52

9 Quoted in Peter Manual – *Cassette Culture: Popular Music and Technology in North India*, 1993, p. 12

10 Eugene Chadbourne – 'My Recording Career: LPs and Cassettes', in: James (ed.) – *Cassette Mythos*, 1992, p. 59

11 Hebdige 1987, p. 141

12 Mike Bouchet – 'Joep van Liefland: Cultural Anthro-Nonapologist', in: Oliver Zybok (ed.) – *Joep van Liefland: Mastertape*, 2017, p. 102

13 Steve Jones – 'The Cassette Underground', in: Robin James (ed.) – *Cassette Mythos*, 1992, p. 6 f.

14 Dan Fioretti – 'What Do You Do With Them Tapes', in: Robin James (ed.) – *Cassette Mythos*, 1992, p. 18

15 1986-12-12 Brixton Academy – 'Big Al' version, http://www.smithstorrents.co.uk/viewtopic.php?p=22789&sid=6ee2e765621492893ba0f55764a83adb

16 'Sen. Sieroty To Investigate What Happens After Blank Tape Sale', in: *Billboard*, 7 April 1979, p. 10

17 Chang 2011, p. 127

18 Michel Foucault – 'The Challenge of the Opposition', in: Janet Afary and Kevin B. Anderson (eds.) – *Foucault and the Iranian Revolution: Gender and the Seductions of Islam*, 2005, p. 219

19 Jude Rogers – 'Total rewind: 10 key moments in the life of the cassette', in: *The Guardian*, 30 August 2010

20 Interview with Don Campau, *The Living Archive of Underground Music*, 2 November 2011

21 Ben Tobin – 'Music: the vinyl frontier', YouGov.co.uk, 8 August 2016

22 Quoted in Oliver Zybok (ed.) – *Joep van Liefland: Mastertape*, 2017, p. 23

23 Theodor Adorno – 'Bibliographical Musings', in: *Notes to Literature*, 1992, p. 28

24 John Cage – 'Experimental Music', in: *Silence*, 2015, p. 9

25 Quoted in Karin Bijsterveld and Annelies Jacobs – 'Storing Sound Souvenirs: The Multi-Sited Domestication of the Tape Recorder', in: Karin Bijsterveld and José van Dijck (eds.) – *Sound Souvenirs: Audio Technologies, Memory and Cultural Practices*, 2009, p. 29

26 See Luz María Sánchez – *Technological Epiphanies: Samuel Beckett and Sound Technologies*, 2016, translation by John Z. Komurki

27 William Burroughs – 'The Electronic Medium', 2015, p. 13

28 See Robin James (ed.) – *Cassette Mythos*, p. 87 ff.

29 Ludovico 2012, p. 77

30 Krukowski 2017, p. 208, then p. 121; emphases, but not ellipses in the original

31 Jacques Derrida – *Paper Machine*, 2005, p. 42

32 Krukowski 2017, p. 89

33 'You Are Cyborg'; interview with Hari Kunzru, 2 January 1997

34 Krukowski 2017 p. 205, then p. 207

35 Paul Hegarty – 'The Hallucinatory Life of Tape', in: *Culture Machine*, vol. 9, 2007

Cassette Cultures
Past and Present of a Musical Icon

The Deutsche Nationalbibliothek lists this publication in the
Deutsche Nationalbibliografie; detailed bibliographic data are
available on internet at http://dnb.dnb.de

ISBN 978-3-7165-1848-9

© English edition 2019 Benteli, imprint of Braun Publishing AG,
Salenstein, www.benteli.ch

A Vetro Editions project, www.vetroeditions.com
© Vetro Editions
© Texts: John Z. Komurki (unless otherwise credited)

Author
John Z. Komurki

Curated by
Luca Bendandi, Vetro Editions

Design
Luca Bendandi
Taís Massaro